# Christian Faith Perspectives in Leadership and Business

**Series Editors**
Kathleen Patterson
School of Global Leadership and Entrepreneurship
Regent University
Virginia Beach, VA, USA

Doris Gomez
Regent University
Virginia Beach, VA, USA

Bruce E. Winston
Regent University
Virginia Beach, VA, USA

Gary Oster
Regent University
Virginia Beach, VA, USA

This book series is designed to integrate Christian faith-based perspectives into the field of leadership and business, widening its influence by taking a deeper look at its foundational roots. It is led by a team of experts from Regent University, recognized by the Coalition of Christian Colleges and Universities as the leader in servant leadership research and the first Christian University to integrate innovation, design thinking, and entrepreneurship courses in its Masters and Doctoral programs. Stemming from Regent's hallmark values of innovation and Christian faith-based perspectives, the series aims to put forth top-notch scholarship from current faculty, students, and alumni of Regent's School of Business & Leadership, allowing for both scholarly and practical aspects to be addressed while providing robust content and relevant material to readers. Each volume in the series will contribute to filling the void of a scholarly Christian-faith perspective on key aspects of organizational leadership and business such as Business and Innovation, Biblical Perspectives in Business and Leadership, and Servant Leadership. The series takes a unique approach to such broad-based and well-trodden disciplines as leadership, business, innovation, and entrepreneurship, positioning itself as a much-needed resource for students, academics, and leaders rooted in Christian-faith traditions.

More information about this series at
http://www.palgrave.com/gp/series/15425

Steven Crowther

# Biblical Servant Leadership

An Exploration of Leadership for the
Contemporary Context

palgrave
macmillan

Steven Crowther
Grace College of Divinity
Fayetteville, NC, USA

Christian Faith Perspectives in Leadership and Business
ISBN 978-3-319-89568-0          ISBN 978-3-319-89569-7    (eBook)
https://doi.org/10.1007/978-3-319-89569-7

Library of Congress Control Number: 2018944428

Cover illustration: ISerg / iStock / Getty Images Plus

Printed on acid-free paper

This Palgrave Macmillan imprint is published by the registered company Springer International Publishing AG part of Springer Nature.
The registered company address is: Gewerbestrasse 11, 6330 Cham, Switzerland

# Contents

**1  The Foundation of Servant Leadership Theory**                      1
Servant Leadership According to Greenleaf                               1
Servant Leadership in Twenty-First-Century Literature                  3
Servant Leadership According to Patterson and Winston                  5
Servant Leadership Research                                            8
The Next Steps in Leadership                                           9
Conclusion                                                            10
References                                                            10

**2  Servant Leadership in Context**                                  13
In the Context of Leadership Theory                                   13
In the Context of Followers                                           14
In the Context of the Business World                                  17
In the Context of the Church World                                    19
In the Global Context                                                 21
Conclusion                                                            22
References                                                            23

**3  The Strengths of Servant Leadership**                            25
Values-Driven Leadership                                              26
Effective and Ethical Leadership                                      28
Servant Leadership and Organizational Culture                         29

| | |
|---|---|
| Servant Leadership and Leadership Development | 30 |
| The Goals of Servant Leadership | 32 |
| Servant Leadership and the Negative | 34 |
| Conclusion | 35 |
| References | 36 |

**4   Servant Leadership in the Old Testament** — **39**

| | |
|---|---|
| Examples of Leaders in the Old Testament | 41 |
| Genesis: Joseph | 41 |
| Exodus 3 and 18: Moses | 44 |
| Esther 4–5: Esther | 51 |
| Instructions for Leaders in the Old Testament | 52 |
| God as the Model Leader in the Old Testament | 53 |
| Pictures of Leaders in the Old Testament | 53 |
| Shepherd: Kings, Priests, Elders | 53 |
| Suffering Servant: Isaiah 52–53 | 54 |
| Levites | 55 |
| The Prophets as Servants: Jeremiah, Ezekiel, Elijah | 56 |
| The Texts of Servant Leadership in the Old Testament | 57 |
| 2 Sam. 17:27–29; 19:31–40; 1 Kings 2:7—Barzillai | 57 |
| 1 Kings 3: Solomon | 58 |
| Nehemiah | 58 |
| 1 Samuel: David and Saul | 60 |
| The Failure of Leadership in the Old Testament | 63 |
| Judges: Samson, Gideon | 63 |
| Prophets: Elisha's Servant | 65 |
| Shepherds Who Failed Jeremiah 23, Ezekiel 34 | 66 |
| The Failure of Moses | 70 |
| Servant Leadership or Shepherd Leadership | 71 |
| Leadership Lessons from the Old Testament | 71 |
| Conclusion | 72 |
| References | 72 |

**5   Servant Leadership in the Life of Jesus** — **75**

| | |
|---|---|
| Instructions About Serving | 76 |
| Mark 10 | 76 |
| Matthew 28 | 82 |

John 13, John 21                                                  84
Luke 7                                                            87
Jesus as the Example of Servant Leadership                        89
  1 Peter 2                                             89
  Phil 2                                                90
Conclusion                                                        93
References                                                        94

**6 Leadership in the New Testament**                             97
Servant Leadership in the Book of Acts                            98
  Barnabas                                              98
  Aeneas                                                99
  Priscilla and Aquila                                 100
  Peter as the Servant Leader                          100
  Instructions to Leaders                              103
Servant Leadership in the Epistles                               105
  Romans and Corinthians                               105
  The Prison Epistles                                  113
  The Pastoral Epistles                                117
  The General Epistles                                 123
  Apocalyptic Servant Leadership                       126
Other Leadership Issues and Models in the New Testament          127
Leadership Lessons from the New Testament                        128
Conclusion                                                       131
References                                                       131

**7 Biblical Servant Leadership**                                135
Biblical Concepts for Servant Leadership                         135
Biblical Love in Leadership                                      141
The Difference and the Cohesion in the Servant
Leadership Models                                                145
Moving from Concept to Application                               146
Application in the Business World                                148
Application in the Church World                                  149
Conclusion                                                       150
References                                                       151

**8  A Call for Biblical Leadership**                                  153
  Existing Research on Biblical Leadership                        153
  Moving on in Biblical Leadership                                154
  Application of Biblical Leadership                              158
  Biblical Leadership: Pioneers or Settlers                      159
  Conclusion                                                     163
  References                                                     165

**Index**                                                        167

# List of Figures

Fig. 5.1  Chiasm from Mark 10:45                                          79
Fig. 6.1  Biblical model of leadership from 1 Timothy 3:1–7              122
Fig. 7.1  Biblical servant leadership                                   148
Fig. 8.1  Biblical leadership                                           157

# List of Tables

Table 4.1  Repetitive and progressive texture of scenes of Exodus 3:1–15    45
Table 4.2  Contrasts of shepherding from bad leadership                      69
Table 5.1  Mark 10:42–45 patterns                                           79
Table 5.2  The progression of the life of Christ                            92
Table 6.1  Contrasts for shepherd leaders                                  102
Table 6.2  The inner texture of I Timothy 3:1–7                            119

# Introduction

Though leadership has been an issue of discussion for many centuries, as well as among recent researchers, there has been little agreement on the description of leadership. In the twentieth century, leadership has been a topic of study by researchers with no consensus on the definition of leadership, but only that it concerns influence in the accomplishment of group objectives (House, Hanges, Javidian, Dorfman, & Gupta, 2004). This vast array of differing conceptions of leadership has created a bewildering body of literature with differences from one writer to another in the field of leadership (Yukl, 2012). However, in the midst of this discussion has entered the concept of spirituality as found in the Hebrew and Christian Scriptures and its impact on leadership. Weber (1968) based his concepts for religious leadership upon the lives of certain religious leaders, like Moses, Buddha, Mohammed, and Jesus. Nevertheless, McClymond (2001) found it striking that there was not much discussion of religious leadership among scholars in the twentieth century. Yet, with the turn of the twenty-first century, there has been a turn to spirituality in leadership studies (Bekker, 2008). This turn to spirituality has included the development of theories of leadership with a spiritual component like spiritual leadership (Fry, 2003), servant leadership (Patterson, 2003), and authentic leadership (Avolio, Gardner, Walumbwa, & May, 2004; Klenke, 2007). This turn to spirituality in leadership studies has also included distinctively Christian leadership models like kenotic leadership

(Bekker, 2006). This is not to say that spirituality and servant leadership are the same. In addition, this does not mean that this turn to spirituality is necessarily Christian with a focus on biblical foundations for leadership. Servant leadership exists without the issues of spirituality. However, this turn to spirituality with a focus on biblical concepts could inform not only servant leadership but other forms of leadership as well. Many have discussed leadership in the context of Christianity and Scripture including Augustine, Martin Luther, and the writers of the Christian Scriptures (Guinness, 2000). Some of the writers of Christian Scriptures who addressed leadership were Mark, Paul, and Peter. Research has been done by some authors on the impact of the writers of Christian Scripture and the ministry of Jesus (Bekker, 2006; Self, 2009; Zarate, 2009) on contemporary leadership. Clinton (2012) developed leadership emergence theory based upon his broad study of leaders in the Hebrew and Christian Scriptures as well.

Nevertheless, this source for leadership theory needs further investigation for at least two reasons. First, this is a new area of research for contemporary leadership that has only gained ascendancy since the turn of the century. Second, this is a broad source for research in the area of leadership and much more needs to be done to develop profundity as well as breadth from this rich resource of the Hebrew and Christian Scriptures.

In response to this need, some scholarly journals have begun in the twenty-first century, such as *The Journal for Biblical Perspectives in Leadership* and *The Journal of Religious Leadership*, to promote research in the areas of Christian Scriptures, Christian spirituality, and leadership. In this area of research, there is much to be examined and gained for contemporary leadership development and understanding. In contemporary leadership, one result of neglecting the spiritual dimension in leadership is a void of values, and in response to many public failures, a movement of spirituality is awakening in businesses across the country (Gibbons, 2008). In the context of this nexus of the Scriptures and leadership, possibly there is a way to discover new models for effective leadership for the future. Many contemporary theories of leadership have focused primarily on behavior like leadership practices (Kouzes & Posner, 2017), transformational leadership, and the skills or style approach (Northouse, 2015), while others focused on the culture of the organization (Cameron & Quinn, 2011) including an emphasis on changing leadership behavior.

Yet, leadership is not just behaviors or styles; it involves internal issues as well. Internal issues such as character. Character is central to good leadership and character is the inner form that makes a person who he/she is and it provides the leader's deepest source of bearings (Guinness, 2000). The issue of personhood or ontology comes to the fore in this discussion and involves spirituality particularly as found in the Christian Scriptures. This is important in that leadership as seen in the Scriptures is ontological in that leadership proceeds from the being of the person and not just the behavior of the person. Though those like Machiavelli (1515/2016) said that internal issues such as character and integrity are not important components of leadership, writers of the Scriptures disagree. In 1 Peter, Peter exhorted the leaders to follow the example of Jesus—Jesus set the example of servant leadership, but this concept permeates the pages of both Old and New Testaments. Therefore, the writings of the Scripture need thorough examination for understanding teaching concerning servant leadership and leadership in general and its proper appropriation for contemporary contexts. In this search, it is possible that even better models for leadership could be discovered from the wisdom of antiquity.

Leadership studies do not generally embrace theology in the process of research (Ayers, 2006). However, in the past, theology or research from the Scriptures has been a valuable source of research. Medieval theologians believed that theology was the queen of the sciences (i.e. of the domains of knowledge) and philosophy was her handmaid; but in our day, theology has been largely banished from the university (DeWeese & Moreland, 2005). Theology has fallen from this place of prominence to be replaced by pragmatism and empiricism. Instead of searching for truth in theological foundations, truth is now sought in answering questions of function. Does it work in accomplishing the objectives? If something accomplishes certain determined objectives, then it is assumed that it is true and this truth is used for developing a theory. Nevertheless, this is quite Aristotelian that truth lies in the physical world. It would be more productive to find truth then apply it to the physical world, a move from internals to externals. While this sounds Platonic, it is not Platonic thinking that drives this as much as theological thinking. Thinking theologically is a view from the perspective of divine intention and prerogative rather than a view from below which is anthropological—an effort to find truth as it happens—and is troubled by misshapen self-issues. Many times science asks for an outside objective viewpoint, but is that possible when we study ourselves and we are the researcher and the researched? Theology from Scripture lifts us out of this research circle so we can catch a glimpse from above concerning the human issue of leadership. Nevertheless, theology is not unacquainted with the necessity of circularity since no quest for truth can escape from the necessity of this hermeneutic circle, linking the encounter with reality to an interpretive point of view, so science and theology are joined in a relationship of mutual illumination and correction (Polkinghorne, 2007). Scripture must be brought back to the research arena, not to displace science, but as a partner in a search for truth that is more than empirical. Science and theology are both concerned with the search for truth, and they share common ways of approaching this search for understanding as well as sharing a common conviction that there is truth to be sought (Polkinghorne, 2007). Therefore, it is in this convergence of science or research and theology from Scripture that truth is sought for leadership in the contemporary setting.

The ramifications for leadership from the principles of Scripture are significant. This is a way of leadership and leadership development that is not only countercultural but also sensitive to eternal issues of theology that are important. This leadership in Scripture is specifically designed for leading the church in antiquity and in contemporary settings as well. The implications are that if the biblical foundation for leadership could be found, it could bring new ground for effectiveness. This then would have implications for leadership in multiple contexts in the twenty-first century including business, education, and government settings as well as in the church.

# References

Avolio, B. J., Gardner, W. L., Walumbwa, W. O., & May, D. (2004). Unlocking the Mask: A Look at the Process by Which Authentic Leaders Impact Follower Attitudes and Behaviors. *Leadership Quarterly, 15*(6), 801–823.

Ayers, M. (2006). Towards a Theology of Leadership. *Journal of Biblical Perspectives in Leadership, 1*, 3–27.

Bekker, C. J. (2006). *The Philippians Hymn (2:5–11) as an Early Mimetic Christological Model of Christian Leadership in Roman Philippi*. Paper presented at the Servant Leadership Research Roundtable.

Bekker, C. J. (2008). The Turn to Spirituality and Downshifting. In F. Ghandolphi & H. Cherrier (Eds.), *Downshifting: A Theoretical and Practical Approach to Living a Simple Life*. Hyderabad, India: ICFAI Press.

Cameron, K. S., & Quinn, R. E. (2011). *Diagnosing and Changing Organizational Culture: Based on the Competing Values Framework*. San Francisco: Jossey-Bass.

Clinton, J. R. (2012). *The Making of a Leader*. Colorado Springs, CO: NavPress.

DeWeese, G. J., & Moreland, J. P. (2005). *Philosophy Made Slightly Less Difficult*. Downers Grove, IL: InterVarsity Press.

Fry, L. W. (2003). Toward a Theory of Spiritual Leadership. *The Leadership Quarterly, 14*(6), 693–727.

Gibbons, S. (2008). Spiritual Formation: The Basis for All Leading. *Inner Resources for Leaders, 1*, 1–9.

Guinness, O. (2000). *When No One Sees: The Importance of Character in an Age of Image*. Colorado Springs, CO: NavPress.

House, R. J., Hanges, P. J., Javidian, M., Dorfman, P. W., & Gupta, V. (2004). *Culture, Leadership, and Organizations: The GLOBE Study of 62 Societies*. Thousand Oaks, CA: Sage.

Klenke, K. (2007). Authentic Leadership: A Self, Leader, and Spiritual Identity Perspective. *International Journal of Leadership Studies, 3*(1), 68–97.

Kouzes, J. M., & Posner, B. Z. (2017). *The Leadership Challenge: How to Make Extraordinary Things Happen in Organizations*. Hoboken, NJ: John Wiley and Sons).

Machiavelli, N. (2016). *The Prince* (W. K. Marriott, Trans.). Retrieved from www.gutenberg.org/files/1232/1232-h/1232-h.htm (Original Work Published 1515).

McClymond, M. J. (2001). Prophet or Loss? Reassessing Max Weber's Theory of Religious Leadership. In D. N. Freedman & M. J. McClymond (Eds.), *The Rivers of Paradise: Moses, Buddha, Confucius, Jesus, and Muhammed as Religious Leaders*. Grand Rapids, MI: William B. Eerdmans Publishing Company.

Northouse, P. G. (2015). *Leadership: Theory and Practice* (Thousand Oaks, CA: Sage).

Patterson, K. A. (2003). *Servant Leadership: A Theoretical Model*. Paper presented at the Servant Leadership Roundtable.

Polkinghorne, J. (2007). *Quantum Physics and Theology: An Unexpected Kinship*. New Haven, CT: Yale University Press.

Self, C. (2009). Love and Organizational Leadership: An Intertexture Analysis of 1 Corinthians 13 (Doctoral dissertation). *Dissertation Abstracts International: SectionA, 70*(10). (UMI No. 337775).

Weber, M. (1968). *Economy and Society: An Outline of Interpretive Sociology.* New York, NY: Bedminster Press.

Yukl, G. A. (2012). *Leadership in Organizations.* Englewood Cliffs, NJ: Prentice-Hall.

Zarate, M. (2009). The Leadership Approach of Jesus in Matthew 4 and 5 (Doctoral dissertation). *Dissertation Abstracts International: SectionA, 70*(10). (UMI No. 3377777).

# 1

# The Foundation of Servant Leadership Theory

The ideas and concepts for servant leadership have been around for centuries in different forms. Even when Aristotle and later Aquinas discussed leadership, they pondered the concepts of virtues as an important component of human life and leadership. Other philosophers such as Plato discussed leadership but with some different ideas that became mainstream ideas for ruling and power. This focus on power carried the day in leadership thinking with concepts of leadership like in Machiavelli's *The Prince* that endorsed a power center to leadership. This power focus on leadership developed over the centuries, while in other contexts alternative concepts for leadership became part of the lived experiences of leaders. Diverse concepts for leaders were lived and developed, but the power focus of leadership rose to ascendancy over the years.

## Servant Leadership According to Greenleaf

In the 1970s, in the midst of a hotbed of leadership theory development, Robert Greenleaf proposed an idea about the servant being the leader. According to Greenleaf (2002), his book on servant leadership was written through a process of 20 years of talks and articles with the

© The Author(s) 2018
S. Crowther, *Biblical Servant Leadership*, Christian Faith Perspectives in
Leadership and Business, https://doi.org/10.1007/978-3-319-89569-7_1

hope and design that leaders would learn to serve their followers with skill, understanding, and spirit. This idea grew into a concept of leadership in the writings of Greenleaf that was developed and popularized in the writings of Greenleaf and later with several other authors like Larry Spears. Greenleaf (2002) believed that there were students who were looking for a better way to lead and there were others as well like trustees and clergy in the churches who wanted more effective models for leadership. He introduced this way of leading as leading as a servant. He summarizes his concept of this type of leader as one who is servant first and this begins with the natural feeling that one wants to serve but then there is a conscious choice from there that one wants to lead (Greenleaf, 2002). The movement then is not from leading to serving but from serving to leading.

This way of thinking calls for a new kind of leadership model that puts serving others as the top priority including employees, customers, and the community at large and a number of institutions have adopted this servant-leader approach (Spears, 1998). This model has been adopted, discussed, and lived by many in several different fields. As this model has moved from theory to practice, there are others who have developed and adapted this model in many different contexts. There are business leaders who have practiced this model for over 25 years and continue to use it, and this leadership thinking has also influenced many noted writers, thinkers, and leaders (Spears, 1998). The influence and popularity of this way of thinking about leadership grew through the later twentieth century.

In this process, ten characteristics for servant leadership were developed from the writings of this model. The ten characteristics of servant leadership were identified as listening, empathy, healing, awareness, persuasion, conceptualization, foresight, stewardship, commitment to the growth of people, and building community (Spears, 1998). These ten concepts have been researched and developed for use as components of servant leadership with good progress of this model as an effective form of leadership. Servant leadership is viewed as a leadership model that is helpful to organizations by engaging and developing employees and beneficial to followers by engaging people as whole persons with heart, mind, and spirit and it is not limited to Western culture (Van Dierendonck & Patterson, 2010). Greenleaf (2002) even discusses many different contexts in his later chapters as he addresses the issues of cross-cultural leadership.

Then his final chapter turns to the inward journey through the use of poetry and Scripture. Though this is the foundation of servant leadership from an organizational perspective, it has some beginnings of looking to Scripture and particularly the life and ministry of Jesus as a model for leadership. These early concepts have been the fountainhead of much discussion and debate about this philosophy or model or principle of leadership. This thinking began in the 1970s with Robert Greenleaf however; others in the twenty-first century began to think and do research on this way of leading to develop a robust model for effective leadership.

## Servant Leadership in Twenty-First-Century Literature

In the twenty-first century, there was an explosion of literature in many areas of leadership theory and thinking. Some of these areas included virtues and even spirituality as an important component of leadership and leadership development. It was in the early years of this century that authentic leadership was developed as a result of the large scandals in the business world of this time period. As it was developed, there was a spiritual component of this model developed by Klenke (2007). There were other theories as well like adaptive leadership theory (Northouse, 2015).

In this context, there emerged several new ideas and models concerning servant leadership. Just before the turn of the century, Spears (1998) had already been developing some of the concepts of servant leadership in cooperation with other leadership scholars and practitioners such as Stephen Covey, Peter Senge, James Kouzes, Margaret Wheatley, and others. They were exploring different aspects of servant leadership based on the Greenleaf model of leadership.

As the twenty-first century dawned, there were ideas and new priorities in leadership thinking and development. Northouse (2015) described servant leadership as a theory that did not have much empirical evidence with most of the writing on this model being prescriptive rather than focusing on the practice of this way of leadership however; in the twenty-first century, more evidence and research had substantiated and clarified this model. Servant leadership was used by different organizations and endorsed by leadership thinkers and writers, but it still needed further development for use as a theory of leadership. So, the twenty-first century brought an explosion of research in new areas of leadership and leadership development. In this explosion of research, several scholars developed different and diverse attributes and measurements for servant leadership (Barbuto & Wheeler, 2006; Dennis & Bocarnea, 2005; Laub, 1999; Van Dierendonck & Nuijten, 2011; Wong & Davey, 2007). In these studies, the characteristics were both extensive and diverse with a lack of agreement on the characteristics that define servant leadership (Northouse, 2015).

In the midst of this time period, Patterson (2003) developed a model that is virtue based for leadership. This model was further clarified and explained by Winston (2003), who defined and expanded some of the terms used in this model of leadership. The literature concerning servant leadership continues to grow with more variations. However, since this Patterson model is virtue based, it has potential for more development and growth.

In addition, the issues of the twenty-first century have focused on developing ethical models of leadership or at least developing models with ethics in mind for the process of leadership development. This focus of leadership studies in general brings this model of servant leadership to an important place to be examined and developed for use in this present context. The question remains as to how leadership models can be developed that can produce effective and ethical leaders. Ciulla (2014) proposes that leadership needs to be good in two senses, ethical and effective. It is this search for good leadership in these two senses that drives the passion for the development of this model for servant leadership. But is this enough? Is there more beyond this model that serves leaders in their pursuit of good and even great leadership that includes virtues as well as effectiveness? Then the question goes even farther in asking if these are the only two components of good leadership. To answer these questions it takes a deeper look at this Patterson model.

# Servant Leadership According to Patterson and Winston

Some of the foundational ideas for the further development of servant leadership came from Winston and Patterson. Winston gave some new terminology for this construct in using the word *agapao* for the leadership idea of love. Patterson developed a virtue-based model for servant leadership that built upon the ideas of Greenleaf but expanded it. In her model, the virtues of leadership are the central issue however; it is done in such a way that it facilitates the ability to research this theory of leadership for further development.

According to Patterson, servant leadership is based on love (2010). However, there are more virtues that come from this foundation of love producing a virtuous model of leadership. There are seven virtuous constructs in this model of servant leadership. These seven constructs are *agapao* love, humility, altruism, vision, trust, empowerment, and service (Patterson, 2003). These constructs interact with each other ultimately expressing service to others. It begins the process with love or *agapao*. According to Winston (2002), this is the Greek term for moral love; it is to love in a social or moral sense. Fortunately, Greek has several Greek words for different ideas where we use only one word in English. Therefore, it is important to understand this word in this social context. It is where the leader considers the needs of the followers and where the leader considers each person as a total person with unique needs, desires, and wants even learning about the giftings and talents of each follower (Patterson, 2003). Love in this way is important in an organizational setting. Love in leadership is an atmosphere where respect, trust, and dignity are fostered and this is where followers can thrive and this love becomes a force that changes lives of both follower and leader (Van Dierendonck & Patterson, 2010). It is here in the foundation that there can be seen a difference between this model and the Greenleaf model. The Greenleaf model begins with the desire to serve, while the Patterson model begins with moral and social love as the foundation. Does this make enough of a difference? Both are based on the model of serving first. Many of the other discussions on servant leadership have this concept of serving first. However, the Patterson model develops through virtuous constructs rather than behaviors. This then makes it a model that can be developed using internal issues of the person rather than external behaviors. It is then ontological in nature in that it deals with the person of the leader first rather than the external behaviors first. This could be more of a challenge for development, but it makes it more open to research that deals with internal issues like dealt with in Scripture and the issues of character.

The model then moves from the issue of love to humility. This is an often missed but a key ingredient of good leadership. There is a growing call for humility in leadership in spite of the fixation on charismatic appeal for leaders (Morris, Brotheridge, & Urbanski, 2005). Collins (2001) even declares that deep personal humility is one of the only two important ingredients for great leadership. Others have discussed this connection between servant leadership and humility as well (Anderson, 2008; Greenleaf, 2002; Winston, 2002). However, it is important to understand this concept of humility. It is not a low opinion of self. Humility is a personal orientation based upon the willingness to see self accurately putting oneself in perspective with neither self-abasement nor overly positive self-regard (Morris et al., 2005). This concept of humility in connection with leadership is a growing discussion but it fits well within the framework of this model of servant leadership.

Then altruism is the next virtue in this model servant leadership. Altruism is that which benefits another person often involving risk or sacrifice for one's own personal interests (Kaplan, 2000). This virtue would involve the servant leader overcoming significant self-issues like insecurities and overt self-interest. Vision is the next attribute in connection to this model. Vision is rarely considered a virtue. It is an important component for many models of leadership including some of the more contemporary models like transformational leadership. However, this vision becomes a virtue when it is focused on the vision for the follower rather than for the organization. The servant leader's focus is on the individual and this vision is looking forward and seeing the individual as a viable and worthy person and helping that individual become that person (Patterson, 2003). The vision is for the individual and how they can become a better person in a holistic sense, not just as a function at a job. This sets this model apart in that the other models of leadership focus on vision for the strategy of the organization whereas here the vision is to develop the followers in the organization who impact the organization but the goal is the follower first. Servant leaders are focused on their followers seeing them for who they can become and serving them as such whereby the followers are the primary concern (Dennis, Kinzler-Norheim, & Bocarnea, 2010). Servant leadership in this way focuses on the follower through addressing internal issues in the leader.

Trust is the next virtue in servant leadership here in this model and way of doing leadership. Trust is seen as part of the transforming influence of servant leadership by Sendjaya (2010) and he calls unreserved trust one of the ingredients for the transformation of followers in many dimensions. Trust is one of the ingredients produced in an atmosphere of love in leadership (Van Dierendonck & Patterson, 2010). Trust can be seen in two directions. The first direction is the follower trusting the leader but the second direction is the leader trusting the follower. So, trust needs to flow in both directions. However, trust coming from the leader can help develop trust in the follower. This cannot produce trust from the follower without the leader being trustworthy. This is where servant leadership enters the equation. Trust is built upon the other attributes of this model of leadership. When the leader expresses moral love and altruism with good in the heart of the leader for the followers in the context of true humility, the leader builds a solid foundation for trust—trust from the followers. In addition, humble leaders recognize their own shortcoming, and with this revelation, they are able to more readily trust other imperfect individuals. Excellence is not perfection; it is much more than perfection. Perfection is in meeting a certain expectation fully. Nevertheless, excellence is to exceed expectations with a learning process as a result of failures and successes. Excellence, to work correctly, needs to be filled with grace and proper motive. Perfection is a hard task master but excellence is an easy yoke that is filled with expectation instead of fear. So, what is trust? Trust has to do with being predictable and reliable and integrity makes a leader worthy of trust (Northouse, 2015). Trust is the confident relationship built between people who can be relied upon even in difficult situations. People you can trust whether followers or leaders are those who will not throw you under the bus when times are difficult. Collins (2001) says that great leaders are the ones who give credit to followers when all is well and progress is made, but then when there is trouble or hindrance, the leader looks at his/her own contributions as the problem. He calls this humility. However, this is also trust, trust in others and building a foundation of trust from others.

The final virtue and the ultimate virtue in servant leadership is that of service or to serve. The idea of servant is deep in the Judeo-Christian heritage yet society appears to be a low-caring society with some notable servants but they seem to be losing ground to the nonserving people (Spears, 1998). This confusion adds to the dilemma in defining and then living as a servant in contemporary society. Where are the contemporary role models for this important ingredient? This is why Guinness (2003) laments the lack of heroes in our day when people are famous for being famous rather than for some exceptional quality or deed like putting others first. Service is a virtue in giving of oneself with generosity toward others in a variety of ways including giving time, compassion, and even of physical belongings (Patterson, 2003). To serve is to give of self when it is not an obligation; it is not a mandate to be fulfilled but a passion for others to be lived and done with compassion. However, even these words like "compassion" must be used carefully since there are so many who would define these concepts of giving, or serving or even compassion in various ways with practical implications as each definition takes root and heads in different directions. Therefore, the need is seen here for more research in these areas to seek out the nuances and the veracity of this theory. In addition, as these attributes are examined, they will need definitions that can bear the weight of this theory of leadership.

## Servant Leadership Research

As of today, there have been several other authors who have entered this field of research for servant leadership doing research in different cultures and contexts. Research has been done in African nations, in military contexts, and based upon the life and teachings of Jesus. As research has been done, some have begun to develop theories that are sensitive to these contexts, like Wilkes (1998) who developed a concept for leadership based upon the life and teachings of Jesus or Bell (2014) who developed leadership principles from both Old and New Testaments based upon the servant models found in Scripture. Many scholars have worked on developing a model of servant leadership recently. Among these scholars are Patterson (2003) and Winston (2003), but there are others as well like Russell (2001). These scholars have used differing theories and developed different models. In this process, some have begun to look at Hebrew and Christian Scriptures for a foundation for this theory as well as insight for nuances to improve this model of leadership.

## The Next Steps in Leadership

In this endeavor, as some researchers have begun to look at the Hebrew and Christian Scriptures for guidance, there is a call for a more developed theory of leadership. This call is to analyze the best theoretical models in conjunction with divine insights from the text of Scripture. This is a call to think theologically from the perspective of foundations for leadership. Thinking theologically is a view from the perspective of divine intention and prerogative rather than a view from below which is anthropological (which is finding truth as it happens but it is troubled by distorted self-issues). Science asks for an outside objective viewpoint but is that possible when we study ourselves wherein we are the researcher and the researched? Theology lifts us out of this research circle so we can catch a glimpse from above concerning the human issue of leadership. This study expands this research in looking to the Scriptures in cooperation with the science of organizational leadership for divine perspective on servant leadership and its implications for leadership that can be applied in the multiple contexts of the twenty-first century, to the church, government, military, nonprofits, education, and the world of business. Science and theology are both concerned with search for truth. They share common ways of approaching this search for understanding and a common conviction that there is truth to be sought (Polkinghorne, 2007). The question is whether the Scriptures endorse, critique, or expand the concept of servant leadership. Further, the deeper question is whether the Scriptures provide a model of leadership other than servant leadership or that builds beyond this model of leadership.

# Conclusion

There are many models that have built upon the concept of servant leadership as described by Greenleaf (2002). In this research, there is one model that is virtue based developed by Patterson (2003) that will be analyzed in this contemporary context and compared to the Hebrew and Christian Scriptures. The contemporary organizational theory and the examination of Scripture will be brought together in looking for the nuancing, confirming, critiquing, or challenging of this theory. The purpose is to build a biblical construct for leadership using the foundation of servant leadership but moving beyond these concepts to embrace other words and concepts or principles for leadership.

# References

Anderson, J. (2008). *The Writings of Robert K. Greenleaf: An Interpretive Analysis and the Future of Servant Leadership*. Paper presented at the Servant Leadership Research Roundtable.

Barbuto, J. E., Jr., & Wheeler, D. W. (2006). Scale Development and Construct Clarification of Servant Leadership. *Group & Organization Management, 31*(3), 300–326.

Bell, S. (Ed.). (2014). *Servants and Friends: A Biblical Theology if Leadership*. Berrien Springs, MI: Andrews University Press.

Ciulla, J. B. (2014). *Ethics: The Heart of Leadership*. Santa Barbara, CA: ABC-CLIO.

Collins, J. C. (2001). *Good to Great: Why Some Companies Make the Leap—And Others Don't*. New York, NY: Harper Business.

Dennis, R. S., & Bocarnea, M. (2005). Development of the Servant Leadership Assessment Instrument. *Leadership and Organization Development Journal, 25*(8), 600–615.

Dennis, R. S., Kinzler-Norheim, L., & Bocarnea, M. (2010). Servant Leadership Theory: Development of the Servant Leadership Assessment Instrument. In D. Van Dierendonck & K. A. Patterson (Eds.), *Servant Leadership: Developments in Theory and Research* (pp. 169–179). New York, NY: Palgrave Macmillan.

Greenleaf, R. (2002). *Servant Leadership: A Journey into the Nature of Legitimate Power and Greatness.* Mahwah, NJ: Paulist Press.

Guinness, O. (2003). *The Call: Finding and Fulfilling the Central Purpose of Your Life.* Nashville, TN: W Publishing.

Kaplan, S. (2000). New Ways to Promote Proenvironmental Behavior: Human Nature and Environmentally Responsible Behavior. *Journal of Social Issues, 56*(3), 491–508.

Klenke, K. (2007). Authentic Leadership: A Self, Leader, and Spiritual Identity Perspective. *International Journal of Leadership Studies, 3*(1), 68–97.

Laub, J. (1999). Assessing the Servant Organization: Development of the Servant Organizational Leadership (SOLA) Instrument. *Dissertation Abstracts International, 60*(2), 308 (UMI No. 9921922).

Morris, A. J., Brotheridge, C. M., & Urbanski, J. C. (2005). Bringing Humility to Leadership: Antecedents and Consequences of Leader Humility. *Human Relations, 58*(10), 1323–1350.

Northouse, P. G. (2015). *Leadership: Theory and Practice.* Thousand Oaks, CA: Sage.

Patterson, K. A. (2003). *Servant Leadership: A Theoretical Model.* Paper presented at the Servant Leadership Roundtable.

Patterson, K. A. (2010). Servant Leadership and Love. In D. Van Dierendonck & K. A. Patterson (Eds.), *Servant Leadership: Developments in Theory and Research* (pp. 67–76). New York, NY: Palgrave Macmillan.

Polkinghorne, J. (2007). *Quantum Physics and Theology: An Unexpected Kinship.* New Haven, CT: Yale University Press.

Russell, R. F. (2001). The Role of Values in Servant Leadership. *Leadership & Organization Development Journal, 22*, 76–84.

Sendjaya, S. (2010). Demystifying Servant Leadership. In D. Van Dierendonck & K. A. Patterson (Eds.), *Servant Leadership: Developments in Theory and Research* (pp. 39–51). New York, NY: Palgrave Macmillan.

Spears, L. C. (Ed.). (1998). *Insights into Leadership: Service, Stewardship, and Servant Leadership.* New York, NY: Wiley & Sons.

Van Dierendonck, D., & Nuijten, I. (2011). The Servant Leadership Survey: Development and Validation of a Multidimensional Measure. *Journal of Business & Psychology, 26*(3), 249–267.

Van Dierendonck, D., & Patterson, K. A. (Eds.). (2010). *Servant Leadership: Developments in Theory and Research.* New York, NY: Palgrave Macmillan.

Wilkes, C. G. (1998). *Jesus on Leadership: Discovering the Secrets of Servant Leadership from the Life of Christ.* London: Lifeway Press.

Winston, B. (2002). *Be a Leader for God's Sake.* Virginia Beach, VA: Regent University School of Global Leadership & Entrepreneurship.

Winston, B. E. (2003). *Extending Patterson's Servant Leadership Model: Coming Full Circle.* Paper presented at Regent University's Servant Leadership Research Roundtable, Virginia Beach, VA. Retrieved from http://www.regent.edu/acad/global/publications/sl_proceedings/home.shtml

Wong, P. T. P., & Davey, D. (2007). *Best Practices in Servant Leadership.* Regent University Servant Leadership Research Roundtable Proceedings, 2007.

# 2

# Servant Leadership in Context

Servant leadership has been developed and applied in the midst of a very hot economic climate and in the context of an abundance of new leadership research in general. As a result, there are many new ideas to which to compare it for developing the fine nuances of the theory. However, the negative side is that it gets confused with other theories with some similarities.

## In the Context of Leadership Theory

There has been an explosion of research and development in the area of leadership theory from the end of the twentieth century which has intensified with the coming of the twenty-first century. Servant leadership is one of several new and developing theories of leadership beginning with transformational leadership theory but then moving to more current theories like authentic and adaptive theories. Each of these theories has its own distinction, and yet there are a few connections with servant leadership.

Especially in the context of transformational leadership, there is some confusion as to the differences between these growing theories. However, in studying the connection between transformational and servant leadership, there can be some further nuances developed in the understanding

© The Author(s) 2018
S. Crowther, *Biblical Servant Leadership*, Christian Faith Perspectives in
Leadership and Business, https://doi.org/10.1007/978-3-319-89569-7_2

and applying of servant leadership. Transformational leadership is a theory that has been developed and refined through research in many large universities. Servant leadership has been researched and applied in different context even in diverse cultural settings. The distinction between the two can be seen in the particular focus of each theory. Possibly, their similarities are due to their attempt to develop people-oriented leadership styles, but their differences are found in the focus of the leader (Stone, Russell, & Patterson, 2003). He goes on to declare that they both show concern for followers but transformational leaders engage the followers for the organization and servant leaders focus on service to the followers.

This difference can be seen most clearly in the area of vision. Both theories discuss the need for vision. Transformational leaders develop an inspiring vision that captivates and motivates all in the organization, while servant leaders have a vision for the follower and fulfillment for the individual. The focus is different; the process is different though there are some similarities. However, servant leadership focuses on virtues like humility and altruism whereas transformational leadership focuses on inspiration and transformation for the organization and the followers but for the purpose of the mission. In servant leadership, the organization and mission is a focus as a secondary issue as it proceeds from serving others. There is a clear difference, but the question is whether servant leadership can work when the focus is not initially on the organization.

## In the Context of Followers

Servant leadership has a clear focus on followers and one of the issues of servant leadership is in producing more servant leaders. However, the question is whether this kind of leadership will produce servant followers or if servant followers are part of the equation in developing a servant culture in an organization. Greenleaf (2002) discusses followership as a responsible role in the organization in that the follower must take the risk to empower the leader and to trust his/her insight, which will then be a strength-giving element in the organization. Is being a servant in the context of followers an issue for servant leadership and even leadership development? The premise of servant leadership in its foundation is about the desire to become a servant. The servant leader is a servant first, it begins with the natural feeling that one wants to serve, to serve first then this brings one to aspire to lead (Greenleaf, 2002). In the process of becoming a servant leader, it begins with serving before leading. Then is a servant leader first a servant follower, and does a servant leader produce or encourage others to become not only servant leaders but also servant followers?

Traditionally, the world has been viewed from a leader-centric vantage point but what if followership was put at center stage challenging the concept of leaders as the proactive cause and followers as the reactive effect (Kelley, 2008). Followership can become the issue when viewed from the perspective of the follower. Followers make up the majority of an organization and can have an impact on the way the leader leads as well as the way the organization moves into the future. There are different kinds or styles of followers from the passive to the yes people to the alienated or negative ones, then there are the pragmatics who just go with the winds of what is in vogue, and finally there are the star followers who think for themselves but are active and positive (Kelley, 2008). These different types of followers can be found in many different kinds of organizations. However, the question is whether these followers are like this innately or have they been formed by certain leaders or leadership styles, where is the cause and effect here. Or the bigger question is whether there is cause and effect in this relationship? The bigger question is if people are responsible for how they follow and can the followership style be changed?

This is a concept that can be found in Scripture as well. In reality, this was a major issue in the Protestant Reformation in the teaching of Martin Luther. One of the major pillars of the Reformation was called the priesthood of all believers. The clergy-centric model of the middle ages in the church developed a deep dependency for what was called the laity (translated followers) upon the clergy (translated leaders). This dependency meant that the followers had to depend upon the leaders for every aspect of salvation. Inevitably, this gave great amounts of control to the leaders over the everyday lives of the followers. Martin Luther came along and said that every person was a priest. In other words, everyone could connect to God individually and even help others in walking with the Lord. This revolutionized the church and even society.

Nevertheless, this concept did not go very deep into the culture of the new church and it was not long before the church returned to its leader-centric habits.

What does the Scripture have to say on this issue? This is directly addressed in Ephesians 4:11–16. In this pericope, it is the Lord who gives gifts to individuals to lead as apostles, prophets, evangelist, pastors, or teachers. However, they were to use these gifts of leadership in a very specific way. It was to equip and train others or the followers to do the work of serving others and building the community until all, leaders and followers, can become unified, mature, and growing up by building each other up in love. The job of the leader is to focus on and develop the follower to the point that the follower is a powerhouse of service, growth, and maturity then together they bring growth to others in love. Too many churches hinder themselves when they think that the leaders are the point of the church. The leaders are not the point; they are the servants. The church is the bride of Christ not the leaders. The leaders are the bridesmaids to prepare the bride. Church leaders many times miss this point of leadership in the church in that it is really about the followers and the followers are the one who make it work. Many times church are not working well in the present context and many think it is the culture that is the hindrance when in reality it is the result of not hearing the Scripture on this issue of leadership and followership. Could this be true in the business world as well? Principles in Scripture are universal and apply whether they are believed or not believed. In this case, it is a concept that is largely ignored but it could be a catalyst for new concepts for organizations and churches that could lead to new eras of growth. What if every church and organization had new passionate advocates in the hundreds and thousands? This would change everything including leadership.

Winston (2003) proposed a model of followership related to servant leadership wherein the virtues model of servant leadership in service to followers created a replica of this virtue model for followers beginning with love and producing the same virtues with the end of service to the leader. This model is intriguing in both its theory and the practical implications. The implication here is that servant leadership produces servant followers. Is it possible as well that servant followers could produce servant leaders? Is there cause and effect here but can it flow both ways in causation? This is an important question but at the very least it implies a servant followership that is different than a general followership in an organization. Servant leadership can produce a servant culture as seen in the application of servant leadership in places like Southwest Airlines. This culture and intentional training produces more servant leaders. Nevertheless, it would be a worthwhile endeavor to produce servant followers and a servant followership culture. To produce this culture, it would take more than classes on servant leadership and followership. Winston (2003) proposes that maturity of the individual is a moderating variable that can increase the intensity of this response of the servant followers to the servant leaders. This is a biblical issue in that maturity is part of the goal of the Christian life as seen in the text from Ephesians 4. The purpose of leaders and followers is to come to maturity in Christ, in essence to grow up, and this maturity in Christ brings maturity in other areas as well, such as in godly character. These concepts of maturity are linked together.

Servant followership is an important issue in servant leadership in several ways. One is that servant leaders can produce servant followers producing a cycle of love and serving with maturity as part of the growth process. Two is that even servant leaders need to come back to the foundation that is about the followers and equipping them and three is that servant followers could possibly even help to produce servant leaders. Biblically, followers are the issue not the by-product of ministry. As servant leaders focus on followers not just in producing servant leaders but also in producing servant followers, this process of personal and organizational growth can be greatly enhanced.

## In the Context of the Business World

Servant leadership has been applied and researched in the business world in both for profit and nonprofit sectors as well. Greenleaf began to do his research in AT&T in the clearly for profit business world. However, it is not just here but also in government and military sectors that this model has been applied with good results. Greenleaf (2002) described servant leadership as beginning with the natural desire to serve and then he applied and discussed it in the context of the business world as well as the education and even the church world. The classic example and the oft-repeated one is of Southwest Airlines where the concept of servant leadership begins with the CEO but then it is part of the culture of the organization as well. Southwest Airlines has long been known for setting and achieving incredible record of performance as an organization though many have doubted their ability to keep this model of leadership as they grow, but they have done so while increasing to 35,000 employees (McGee-Cooper & Trammel, 2010). This is but one example. Laub (2010) says that many organizations have taken up the banner of servant leadership, which is the understanding and practice of leadership placing the good of the follower over the self-interest of the leader. These organizations are varied and diverse yet they promote, train, and model servant leadership that fits into the broad definition of servant leadership.

There are businesses that are not serving well but much of the problem is in the attitudes, concepts, and expectations regarding business held by society, however; work exists for the person to provide meaningful work as it provides services or products and thereby the business becomes a serving institution (Greenleaf, 2002). Businesses then can be led by servant leaders who provide vision for the organization, but they do so by helping the followers fulfill their own personal call and purpose in the mission of the organization. It has to do with organizational fit and individual calling. Servant leaders help individuals find their personal call in life which is related to their talents, gifts, even their personalities, and inclinations. With this fit between person and mission or business, the followers are served in deeply personal ways that impact their motivation, presence, and even their joy in life. Organizations, even profit organizations can be led by servant leaders who provide service to followers, peers, partners in the business world, customers, and society at large.

Servant leaders develop organizations that are in the business of growing people who become stronger, healthier, more self-reliant, competent, and autonomous while also making and selling at a profit things that people want to buy to be able to pay for the business (Greenleaf, 2002). This is a change in focus. It is a change in attitude, and it is catching on in more and more organizations. TDI is one of the earliest businesses to adopt servant leadership and this heating and plumbing business has been using servant leadership with required servant leadership training since the 1970s (Spears, 1998). Melrose (1995) as the CEO of the Toro Company implemented servant leadership in 1981 producing a book on his journey to leading by serving. There are several instruments that have been established for measuring servant leadership such as the OLA, and these have been used to measure servant leadership and its impact in several companies in the automotive industry and in addition this instrument has been used in health care, law enforcement, and manufacturing contexts (Laub, 2010). There were servant leader-led organizations in these studies which then compared issues like job satisfaction and absenteeism finding these servant organizations made a significant positive difference in these areas (Laub, 2010). There are a growing number of businesses that have adopted servant leadership and have developed programs for developing servant leaders as a model for leadership for the business. Businesses are finding good results with servant leadership with some having used this model for over 25 years like TDI. This trend has continued into the twenty-first century with several instruments developed for measuring, reporting, and developing servant leadership in organizations. Many of these organizations that are using these instruments for improvement are profit businesses. Servant leadership has found its place in the business world in spite of society's perception of the world of business. Possibly, as more search out this way of leading there will be more to come.

## In the Context of the Church World

Of course, one area where servant leadership seems to fit well is in the context of the church and Christian ministry. Nevertheless, it is apparent that church leaders are often autocratic rather than servant leaders. This is an area of concern especially in the context of growing research for the effectiveness of servant leadership. So, this area needs further development in its connection with Jesus and His teachings since He is the ultimate leader in the church. Jesus was the first to endorse serving as leading in Mark 10. However, this also raises the question of whether Jesus taught servant leadership or transformational leadership or another model of leadership. This question will be more fully addressed in Chap. 5 on Jesus' teaching and model of leadership.

Much of the time the church follows culture in forms, styles, and in leadership. The Bible gives us instruction in many areas where the church can lead the culture or at least use some of the grace provided by God to provide a different model. This is particularly true in the area of leadership. Leadership is an arena that God has provided insight since the beginning of humanity. Christian leadership through the centuries has followed many different models of leadership and presently follows either contemporary models or a model that says teaching theology is enough for leadership. It is important that the church begin to embrace some of these insights and models for leadership. There is a need for a new pattern of leadership. Is this model found in biblical servant leadership or is it a related form of leadership and how do we bring this into the church in the midst of a troubled culture filled with distorted self-issues?

Churches are needed to serve the large number of people who need help for healing and wholeness however; the churches do not seem to be serving well, but if the leaders can become servant leaders, the churches can be exemplars for other organizations (Greenleaf, 2002). He is not the only one that is concerned about the state of the churches and their position in society at large. A particular type of leadership is needed then for churches. An important aspect of churches is their relevance to the culture, but can this relevance to the culture be held in proper tension with the biblical foundation needed for ministry and leadership? The modern growing churches employ insights from the behavioral sciences for evangelism and these churches have been deeply impacted by modernity (Guinness, 1993). These aspects of church leadership make them culturally relevant to Western society. However, the endless pursuit of relevance leads only to transience and burnout. The church needs an effective way of leading that is relevant yet transcultural and transgenerational. We need these kind of leaders and concepts of leadership in churches wherein the churches serve well the people of the communities. The sociology of religion literature suggests that there are important insights to be gained by applying institutional theories to religious organizations and religious scholars concerned with organizations have identified the location of authority and the system of governance as some of the most common dimensions of religious organizations (Packard, 2008). There are concepts and principles that the church can learn from organizational leadership theory. However, this is not the only source for the church and the church leaders must use these concepts with wisdom and insights that are uniquely part of the foundation of the church and its mission. Some of the principles important for church growth according to some in the church growth/mega church movement are pastoral leadership effectiveness (Wagner, 1985), leadership and transitions (Fletcher, 2006), and developing several key characteristics including empowering leadership (Schwarz, 1996). What is this empowering leadership? Is it servant leadership? At the very least, servant leadership in concept was endorsed by Jesus as a path to greatness in leading.

It is not only the church that can benefit from servant leadership it is also the nonprofit ministries of all different types and sizes. By their very nature, these organizations exist for a purpose other than the profit motive. Part of the drive behind these organizations is their mission. The mission in this nonprofit world can vary, and even the ministries affiliated with the Christian movement can vary in scope and mission. Yet, they all are motivated by a purpose that is a higher purpose and not a self-focused purpose; otherwise they would not be nonprofit organizations. This then is a fertile ground for servant leadership. The institution that becomes distinguished in the contemporary world will have learned to act in a serving way with great economy of resources, both human and material, while being guided by purpose on the path to a better society (Greenleaf, 2002). This better society can begin with effective leaders becoming servant leaders committed to the growth of people beginning with those in the organization. This can then be applied to helps agencies, mission agencies, church development agencies, and other organizations that have been founded to help others around them in society.

## In the Global Context

The question arises as to whether this way of leading can be applied in global contexts. In high authoritarian cultures, the very word "servant" is a problem. There are some areas of the world where it is an insult to be considered a servant in any form. In addition, there are those who have been forced into servanthood or slavery and in this context servant leadership could be and is resisted. So, this asks the question of whether this model can be applied cross-culturally in some of these areas where there are deep cultural resistances to the concept of servant. This model has been researched and tested in some of these contexts with good results but it takes large amounts of explanation for the theory and its application. We must look for a way ahead for this issue since the principles appear to be universal.

The study of servant leadership has moved from theory to model development to empirical research but most of this has been done in North America and Europe however; newer studies have found servant leadership acceptance and endorsement of servant leadership concepts in Africa and Latin America with some acceptance among pastors in Asia (Irving, 2010). This is just a beginning but more research is being done to be able to bring this model into diverse cultural contexts. Serrano (2006) found that in Panama this theory was not only accepted it was also practiced throughout the culture. Though this is understood to be a Western model, it is growing around the world today with studies in Latin America and China showing servant leadership from these cultural perspectives (Ertel, 2017). Global leadership is an important issue today in our newly connected global society and servant leadership is beginning to show up in many non-Western locations. Concepts of servant leadership have been identified in at least one major worldview on every continent and most worldviews give a high place to the role of servant (Ertel, 2017). There is more work to be done in the global aspect of servant leadership. Nevertheless, there is growing evidence that at the very least there is an understanding and acceptance of the concepts of servant leadership in various cultural contexts with some evidence of the practice of this model of leadership.

## Conclusion

Servant leadership is currently being adopted, researched, developed, and explored in many contexts across cultural and organizational lines. Some have been using and developing servant leadership for more than 25 years, while others have just begun to explore the concept. In addition, servant followership is a concept that needs further development in both research and practice. However, the enactment of servant leadership must take on culturally contingent characteristics to be effective and to follow the heart of the model in being follower focused and servant oriented (Irving, 2010). So, in some areas of the world it needs to be adapted to the language of the people in ways that are congruent but not exactly the same in terminology. This is called dynamic equivalence. It is looking for the same overall concept while adjusting the language so it is heard by the listener. It is similar in many ways to language translation. In translating from one language to another, the goal is understanding more than word for word exactness. Since languages are formed differently and the concepts are carried in different ways, adjustments must be made for effective understanding. The best theory of translation is one that remains faithful to both the original and receptor languages but when something has to "give" it is in favor of the receptor language without losing the original meaning, this is functional or dynamic equivalence (Fee & Stuart, 2014). An example would be calling Jesus the bread of Life when speaking to Eskimos. Early on they did not use bread and this would be difficult for them to understand. Another example is that among one Brazilian tribe they had no word for leader so an equivalent was found with some explanation. One possible word to be used in other cultures would be that of "steward" and though it is an old word it is a biblical word for the "lead servant." This adaptation can take place through careful analysis and research of the cultures and servant leadership. Servant leadership has found its place in the worlds of business, church, and across cultures as well as in other contexts. Nevertheless, it needs continued development, research, and application to different contexts. This is a call for more work and even more nuanced work on this model of leadership in the areas of research, development, and expansion.

# References

Ertel, S. R. (2017). Why Servant Leadership? *Servant Leadership Theory and Practice, 4*(2), 13–26.

Fee, G., & Stuart, D. (2014). *How to Read the Bible for All It's Worth: A Guide to Understanding the Bible*. Grand Rapids, MI: Zondervan.

Fletcher, M. (2006). *Overcoming Barriers to Growth*. Bloomington, MN: Bethany House Publishers.

Greenleaf, R. (2002). *Servant Leadership: A Journey into the Nature of Legitimate Power and Greatness*. Mahwah, NJ: Paulist Press.

Guinness, O. (1993). *Dining with the Devil: The Mega Church Movement Flirts with Modernity*. Grand Rapids, MI: Baker Book House.

Irving, J. (2010). Cross-Cultural Perspectives on Servant Leadership. In D. Van Dierendonck & K. A. Patterson (Eds.), *Servant Leadership: Developments in Theory and Research* (pp. 118–129). New York, NY: Palgrave Macmillan.

Kelley, R. (2008). Rethinking Followership. In R. Riggio, I. Chaflen, & J. Lipman-Blumen (Eds.), *The Art of Followership: How Great Followers Create Great Leaders and Organizations* (pp. 5–16). San Francisco, CA: Jossey-Bass.

Laub, J. (2010). The Servant Organization. In D. Van Dierendonck & K. A. Patterson (Eds.), *Servant Leadership: Developments in Theory and Research* (pp. 105–117). New York, NY: Palgrave Macmillan.

McGee-Cooper, A., & Trammel, D. (2010). Servant Leadership Learning Communities: Incubators for Great Places to Work. In D. Van Dierendonck & K. A. Patterson (Eds.), *Servant Leadership: Developments in Theory and Research* (pp. 130–144). New York, NY: Palgrave Macmillan.

Melrose, K. (1995). *Making the Grass Greener on Your Side*. San Francisco, CA: Berret-Koehler Publishers.

Packard, J. (2008). *Organizational Structure, Religious Belief, and Resistance: The Emerging Church*. Unpublished dissertation, Vanderbily University, Nashville, TN.

Schwarz, C. (1996). *Natural Church Development: A Guide to Eight Essential Qualities of Healthy Churches* (L. McAdam, L. Wollin, & M. Wollin, Trans.). Emmelsbull, Germany: C & P Publishing.

Serrano, M. (2006). Servant Leadership: A Viable Model for the Panamanian Context? *ProQuest Digital Dissertations Database*. (Publication No. 3228983).

Spears, L. C. (Ed.). (1998). *Insights into Leadership: Service, Stewardship, and Servant Leadership*. New York, NY: Wiley & Sons.

Stone, G., Russell, R. F., & Patterson, K. A. (2003). *Transformational Versus Servant Leadership: A Difference in Leader Focus*. Paper presented at the Servant Leadership Roundtable.

Wagner, P. (1985). *Leading Your Church to Growth: The Secret of Pastor/People Partnership in Dynamic Church Growth*. Ventura, CA: Regal Books.

Winston, B. E. (2003). *Extending Patterson's Servant Leadership Model: Coming Full Circle*. Paper presented at Regent University's Servant Leadership Research Roundtable, Virginia Beach, VA. Retrieved from http://www.regent.edu/acad/global/publications/sl_proceedings/home.shtml

# 3

# The Strengths of Servant Leadership

Servant leadership has several components as has been seen earlier in this study. Several of these components combine to create some unique strengths to this model of leadership. The interest in servant leadership is continuing to rise as the idea of the ideal of leadership has changed from the heroic leader to one who gives priority to stewardship, ethics, and collaboration and this new call is for leadership that is virtuous (Van Dierendonck & Patterson, 2010). This type of virtuous leadership that is attentive to the issues of ethics and others is the foundation of servant leadership and fits well with Patterson's (2003) model. There are two important elements in servant leadership theory in that it is person oriented and it deals with the issue of using power well in using power for service (Van Dierendonck & Patterson, 2010). These two areas combine to create an important dynamic in leadership with a focus on followers that develops a context for good motivation to grow. First, the motivation in the leader is concern for others first and this includes followers, clients, customers, partners, and even the community at large. It does not stop there though. This develops good ground in the hearts of these followers for good motivation to grow as well in relationship to others and in relationship to the organization. In leadership and in life motive counts. It is not just how something is done, but it is also why that counts. This motive

© The Author(s) 2018
S. Crowther, *Biblical Servant Leadership*, Christian Faith Perspectives in
Leadership and Business, https://doi.org/10.1007/978-3-319-89569-7_3

issue goes very deep into the soul of the person. Organizational leaders often look for ways to motivate others, such as employees or customers. However, the direct approach of telling or selling works less and less in the twenty-first century. Changing motive in followers may work best by changing motive in the leader first. These strengths in this model could be seen as internal or indirect in their implications. Nevertheless, they are strengths that work well in twenty-first-century organizations and meet the growing desire of people to be included and for leaders to be stewards of mission and power rather than overlords of mission and power.

Servant leadership has tens of thousands adherents over the past quarter of a century providing a framework for helping improve the way others are treated who work in organizations and this way of leading offers hope and guidance for a new era with more caring institutions (Greenleaf & Spears, 1998). This model offers new ways of leading that deal with issues of motive and rethinks the issues of power while developing collaborative and ethical leadership. These strengths give servant leadership an attractiveness for leaders, followers, researchers, and society.

## Values-Driven Leadership

At its core, servant leadership is driven by virtues or deeply held values in the leader. In this way, servant leadership addresses the issues of ontology in the leader. The leader becomes a servant; the leader does not just attach serving behaviors. It is an issue of the soul or the person and even of their worldview or of their sense of reality. It is deeply embedded in the person, in the character of the person. Character is internally who one is in the soul, the *ontos* of the person and it is the internal gyroscope in making decisions (Guinness, 2000). Values are part of who one is as a person, in the soul, or the internal parts of the person. Then these values influence every aspect of a person's life including judgments, responses, and commitments serving as guides for actions and decisions (Kouzes & Posner, 2017). These values are at the core of servant leadership including issues that have already been discussed like humility, love, altruism, and trust. Then the vision of this model is directed at others as part of virtue in that it is not self-focused. Service and empowerment are then the products of these virtues. These last two are virtuous constructs in that they are other focused and proceed out of the other four virtues.

Then, since this way of leading is very person oriented for the leader and focused on the other person, it is very personal. Yet, it can be applied in large group settings as well as small ones. Aristotle discussed four virtues to become a flourishing person but servant leadership develops more concepts of virtues that are closer to the concepts of Jesus than to Aristotle or even Aquinas. For Aristotle, there were four cardinal values: courage, justice, prudence, and temperance and by developing and living these virtues one would flourish as a human being (Wright, 2012). Then Aquinas tried to develop these virtues further based upon his understanding of virtue. Nevertheless, the focus here is still on the person as she/he develops these virtues that person flourishes and can be happy. We could compare the virtues of Aristotle with those of servant leadership but that really is not the point. The difference is in the focus or the motive. The focus of the virtues in serving is motives focused on others, whereas the motives of Aristotle are focused on self. This is not to say that virtue development does not need self-work, it does. However, the goal here in serving and leading is focused on others. We see Jesus making this same distinction in Mark 10 when he told the disciples that the path to greatness was paved by learning to become a servant to others. He did talk about self-issues here. He did not rebuke them for wanting to be great; in fact, indirectly, He endorsed it. The path had two parts. First, the leader must become a servant. This is the place of virtue development in the soul which brings ontological change. Then the leader must become servant to all giving her/his life for others. The focus is on becoming for others.

The strength of virtue leadership is that it is foundational in the soul of the person. It is not just what a leader does, but it is more of a process of becoming more and then as a by-product of these particular virtues giving of self in service to others. In reality, leadership is ontological in that it proceeds from who the leader is as a person more than what the leader says. People who follow you become who you are; they do not become who you tell them to become. Think about children and parents. Do children become who their parents tell them to become or follow all of the teachings of the parents? No, children become who their parents are as lived out for them every day of their little lives. Think about it. Back when we had telephones in houses tied with cords to the wall, people could only reach us through those archaic machines. So, after teaching the children not to lie someone would call for the parent and the parent would tell the child, who answered the phone, to tell the caller that the parent was not there. The children get it and then the parent wonders why the teenager lies under pressure later. Many times this is why there is conflict in the home. Teenagers become their parents at the same time that the parents are reevaluating who they are as persons and are not sure that they like what they see in the mirror. Followers become who the leaders are as persons not just what they are told to do or become. This can be a strength for servant leadership since this model is a virtue theory that develops not the doing of the leader but the character or the *ontos* of the leader, which in turn impacts the followers who are served but then they become these people of virtue since this is the role model.

## Effective and Ethical Leadership

This model looks at the connections between leader and follower as important and aims to facilitate growth in the follower first. In doing this, the leader develops qualities and actions that are other oriented that can be classified as ethical. Ethics then is part of this theory of leadership. Other theories consider ethics as an adjunct to effectiveness but not so with servant leadership. Most leadership development plans that use different leadership theories teach the leaders how to succeed but they do not teach them how to handle this success. This is an internal issue of the person of the leader. Servant leadership uniquely prepares the leader to handle the coming success. The current need for leadership is for leaders who are ethical. This can be seen all around us in our culture. Yet, this seems to be a rather difficult task since when it seems these leaders are found, they cannot stand up to the scrutiny of this concept of ethical leadership. Leadership needs to be good in two way to be good leadership: it must be effective and ethical (Ciulla, 2014). Most theories do not address leadership in this way; they only address the issue of effectiveness. This sets up many successful leaders for disaster. There is a dark underside to successful leadership. That underside is the impact that success has on the human soul. Leaders have been trained to be successful, most of the time. However, they have not been trained in how to handle the success when it comes. If the training in leadership includes development of virtues that are internal, that are issues of character, then there is at least a beginning in dealing with the dilemma of success.

Concerning ethics in the New Testament it can be summed up in one word, the word is "love," the chief of the virtues, and it is no accident that the perfect law of God can be summed up by Jesus in the word of love (Witherington, 2016). Ethics can then be seen to be rooted in virtues especially in the virtue of love. There are many theories of ethics just as there are many theories of leadership. These theories can be discussed under different headings each with a different focus. Egoism is like it sounds in doing the best for self, then there is deontology that is adherence to the rules and utilitarianism that asks about good for the most people (Fedler, 2006). These theories cover some areas of ethics but none of them cover ethics in total. There are other theories as well like consequentialism that looks at the effects of a decision and then finally there is virtue theory that considers the person involved in the action or decision (Fedler, 2006). Here is where we find servant leadership as a virtue theory for leadership but at the same time it impacts ethics. Servant leaders lead with love, they are motivated by love, and this love is a force that is so powerful that it changes lives (Patterson, 2010). Here is where the two senses of good leadership can meet and develop as the servant leader leads with the chief of virtues, love.

## Servant Leadership and Organizational Culture

Servant leadership in the senior levels of an organization has been seen to impact how others interact with each other in the organization. This impacts the culture of the organization. Servant leadership in the higher levels of the organization can even impact the employees' interactions with those outside of the organization. The ideas and the doings of servant leadership transfer into the workings of the organization. It is possible for servant leaders to develop a servant organizational culture. The servant organization is an organization with the characteristics of servant leadership being displayed in the culture of the organization and practiced by leaders and followers (Laub, 1999). It is an organization whose culture has been permeated by the concepts of servant leadership.

In organizational theory, there are four different quadrants of culture each with different attributes and definitions of success. An organization has all four in operation but the question is which one is the high quadrant or the lead that sets the culture or the worldview of the organization. These four quadrants are Hierarchy culture with a focus on order and rules, Adhocracy culture with a focus on innovation, Clan culture with a focus on partnership and family, and then Market culture with a focus on external results (Cameron & Quinn, 2011). Each quadrant brings a certain way of operating and a certain strength to the organization with trade-offs from other weaker quadrants. The best culture is usually contingent on the industry of the particular organization and the kind of economic or social climate around the organization. Organizational culture is the framework of the organization and it is important at all times. Change to organizational culture must be done with wisdom and good counsel. However, the servant organization presents an underlying mindset that can provide a healthy foundation in any of these four cultures (Laub, 2010). Greenleaf (2002) declared that institutions themselves could become servants whether they are big businesses, universities, or churches. These servant institutions are those that develop a servant leadership culture within their organizational culture. Possibly, this servant leadership culture could help bring positive change to the organizational cultures of these institutions as well.

## Servant Leadership and Leadership Development

One of the areas that has not been researched as much as leadership theory is that of how to do leadership development. In this model, leadership development is inherent in the model. This theory is ontological in that it impacts the person of the leader. People in an organization become who the leaders really are for good or ill. All of the teaching on transformational leadership will rarely produce a transformational leader unless there is one who becomes a transformational leader for others to follow. In servant leadership, this is inherent in the model of leading.

Leadership development has been researched as to the most effective ways to develop effective leaders. There are various ways that leader can be developed. Day (2000) distinguishes between leader development as the development of human capital and leadership development as the development of social capital. Leader development focuses on the issues developing the person of the leader whereas leadership development focuses on developing the interactions between people in the organization. Leadership development is enhanced by developing networks and effective interactions between people, both leaders and peers as well as customers. In social capital development, emphasis is on building networked relationships among individuals that enhance cooperation and resource exchange in creating organizational value (Day, 2000). For proper development of leadership in an organization both the individual needs to be trained and equipped in the areas of personal development and then in the area of interacting with others in ways that are successful. Both of these areas are fully present in servant leadership as a model and in practice. The practice of service leadership sets the model for both of these areas to be developed in the followers. According to Day (2000), there are three development processes that involve training for both human and social capital; these are modeling, development assignments, and mentoring during challenging assignments. All three of these can be useful in developing servant leaders but the one that is a focus of servant leadership is that of modeling. Since this is a virtue theory and is based upon the change within the person, there must be a motive or a drawing to this change. This can begin as one is led by a servant leader. This then is a way for training leaders for both the development of human capital and the development of social capital in using those virtues for the good of others.

Kouzes and Posner (2017) articulate five key components for effective leaders and one of these issues is for the leader to become the role model for others to follow. This is good and backed up by much of their research. However, this function as a role model needs to move beyond behaviors to internal issues of the person to have long-term deep impact. Servant leadership is that theory which provides this type of values model, deeply personal model that can have long-term impact. So, servant leaders can produce other servant leaders and it has been shown by Laub (1999) that whole organizations can take on the characteristics of servant leadership. For this to happen, there must be many servant leaders at all levels of the organization. Therefore, it is imperative that servant leaders learn to develop other servant leaders. However, to a point it is inherent in the model. Servants who lead want to produce other servants who lead since this would serve the larger organization and society better. Servant leadership provides means for personal growth and transformation and it encourages everyone to seek opportunities to both serve and lead producing the potential for raising the quality of life throughout society (Spears, 2010). Servant leaders are not deterred by the issues of who has the power or authority or even recognition; they want to serve. Servant leaders can serve as intentional role models for others and expand their ability to serve and in the process develop servant leaders who produce servant organizations. This is not just theory or logical processes; this is reporting that which is already happening at places like Southwest Airlines and TDI. Leaders at Southwest Airlines established an "others first" philosophy in the management of the company then the employees became servant leaders and the company thrived (Northouse, 2015). Leadership development by modeling produces more servant leaders which can cause the company to thrive.

## The Goals of Servant Leadership

Servant leadership focuses on different goals that are person centered rather than organization centered however; these goals still make for a strong model of leadership that impacts both the organization and the community. The goals proceed from the virtues of servant leadership in the leader operating based upon these virtues for the good and the development of the follower and others. Servant leaders put followers first empowering, nurturing, and empathizing with them while helping them develop their full personal capacities and serving for the greater good as well, including society and the organization (Northouse, 2015). The goals of servant leadership are other focused but it is based upon virtues that have been developed in the leader.

The first goal is to become a servant. In the beginning of the discussion of servant leadership, Greenleaf (2002) says that this serving should come from a natural desire to serve. Some do have this natural desire but others need some transformation first possibly through the influence of another servant leader who serves as mentor and role model. Jesus said in Mark 10 that to be great one must become a servant of all not just do serving. This Patterson (2003) model of servant leadership picks up this thought by developing a virtue theory. Virtues are not done as much as developed in the person then they proceed from that person.

Then the second goal is to serve others that are led. The servant leader is servant first taking care that other people's highest priority needs are being served, to help others grow as persons becoming healthier, wiser, freer and to help them become servants themselves (Greenleaf, 2002). This service proceeds from the virtues that begin with love and come through the other virtues of humility and altruism along with trust. Then the leader serves the followers through vision for them many times having more confidence and vision for them than they do themselves. Then empowering and serving them. Inside this goal is the goal to help the followers discover and follow their call in life. This call is unique to every person. Yet every person has a call in life that they have unique talents, abilities, and propensities to fulfill (Guinness, 2000). Life can be a drudgery just existing on survival and yet in some ways this has become the standard. Discovering one's call is the key to a full life filled with purpose. Workers can trudge out 30 years doing something because they have to survive or they can live a life of expectation and adventure discovering and fulfilling call and both can happen in the same organization. The difference is leadership. Someone must serve them to find who they are and what they were created to do and then give them ways to walk that path of purpose. The second goal is the follower living a fulfilled and flourishing life while becoming a servant as well.

The final goal is to serve society at large and the organization. The larger issue of the organization is not left out it is simply prioritized lower than the followers. It has already been seen that in the context of servant leadership and servant organizations that organizations prosper. If the organizations do not prosper then we cannot serve each other anymore and we need to go find another place to serve. Leaders and followers want the organization to prosper but as a result of healthy leader and follower issues not in spite of difficult leader and follower issues. Some of the outcomes of servant leadership are improved organizational performance and societal impact with initial research showing servant leadership has an influence on organizational performance (Northouse, 2015). Concerning societal impact it is seen in organizations that serve the community whether they are nonprofit or for profit. One example is churches that serve the needs of the poor in the community. Another is a college or university that allows its staff to use work hours to work in literacy or reading development for those that need help in the community.

These are the goals generally for servant leadership though some examples used a particular model of servant leadership. However, the question remains as to whether servant leaders can meet all of these goals. The further question is whether these are enough goals or the right goals for good leadership. Then the question of the diversity of models in this theory of leadership comes to the surface in asking the question of whether these goals are clear enough and can be met by all of these models. The final question is—is there more? Is there more to this model in the nuances of the model, or is there more to this model in being connected to the different theories that produce different concepts. Finally is the question of the critique and expansion of this model—does it need more work?

## Servant Leadership and the Negative

In the midst of all of these questions, there can be seen some weaknesses in this theory of leadership. One weakness would include the focus of the leader in if the leader focuses on the followers then who will drive the organization. This is the question of organizational performance. We have already seen that the goals include organizational performance but secondary or as a by-product of the first goals that are follower focused. Can an organization thrive with a vision focused on followers and not on the overall mission of the organizations or on strategic futures for the planning and development of the organization? However, it is here as in other places that the Scripture can help us learn how to become a servant leader while driving the organization.

Are there other weaknesses in this model? Northouse (2015) says that some criticisms of this model are that putting others first seems to contradict other important leadership concepts such as directing and concern for production and that researchers are unable to come up with a common framework for this theory of leadership. However, this is not the first theory of leadership that has struggled with diverse concepts for the model. Trait theory is one that still has several frameworks. However, this first concern may have some merit that needs further research and development with proper nuances for the findings. This "putting others first" is a core issue of servant leadership. This question needs to be answered and this is where Scripture can help as well.

## Conclusion

Servant leadership has many important facets and nuances to it as the model exists today. It is founded upon virtues that help answer the question of ethics and leadership or power. It is good leadership in both senses of good, effective, and ethical. Servant leadership interacts with organizational culture in positive ways producing important outcomes for the follower and the organization. Servant leadership also has some unique qualities for developing other leaders in the organization even producing a servant organization. The goals of servant leadership involve virtue development in the leader, a focus on followers to fully develop them as individuals, and a broader goal for the organization and society. However, everything in servant leadership revolves around this focus on followers, even the other two goals. This follower focus is the gravitational center of servant leadership. Then in the final examination though there are weaknesses in this model of leadership that need to be examined, researched, and addressed. The two issues that come to the surface here are the issue of vision and the core issue of the follower focus. Can an organization thrive when the vision is focused on the follower rather than the organization? The second question is similar in questioning whether this "putting others first" can work when there are other leadership qualities that need to be in a theory of leadership like directing people and projects. These questions and others will be discussed as the text of Scripture is examined. The further question now is does Scripture endorse servant leadership and if so, does it expand, contradict, or critique this theory of leadership.

# References

Cameron, K. S., & Quinn, R. E. (2011). *Diagnosing and Changing Organizational Culture: Based on the Competing Values Framework*. San Francisco: Jossey-Bass.

Ciulla, J. B. (2014). *Ethics: The Heart of Leadership*. Santa Barbara, CA: ABC-CLIO.

Day, D. V. (2000). Leadership Development: A Review in Context. *The Leadership Quarterly, 11*(4), 581–613.

Fedler, K. D. (2006). *Exploring Christian Ethics: Biblical Foundations for Morality*. Louisville, KY: John Knox Press.

Greenleaf, R. (2002). *Servant Leadership: A Journey into the Nature of Legitimate Power and Greatness*. Mahwah, NJ: Paulist Press.

Greenleaf, R., & Spears, L. (1998). *The Power of Servant Leadership*. San Francisco, CA: Berrett-Koehler Publishers.

Guinness, O. (2000). *When No One Sees: The Importance of Character in an Age of Image*. Colorado Springs, CO: NavPress.

Kouzes, J. M., & Posner, B. Z. (2017). *The Leadership Challenge: How to Make Extraordinary Things Happen in Organizations*. Hoboken, NJ: John Wiley and Sons.

Laub, J. (1999). Assessing the Servant Organization: Development of the Servant Organizational Leadership (SOLA) Instrument. *Dissertation Abstracts International, 60*(2), 308 (UMI No. 9921922).

Laub, J. (2010). The Servant Organization. In D. Van Dierendonck & K. A. Patterson (Eds.), *Servant Leadership: Developments in Theory and Research* (pp. 105–117). New York, NY: Palgrave Macmillan.

Northouse, P. G. (2015). *Leadership: Theory and Practice*. Thousand Oaks, CA: Sage.

Patterson, K. A. (2003). *Servant Leadership: A Theoretical Model*. Paper presented at the Servant Leadership Roundtable.

Patterson, K. A. (2010). Servant Leadership and Love. In D. Van Dierendonck & K. A. Patterson (Eds.), *Servant Leadership: Developments in Theory and Research* (pp. 67–76). New York, NY: Palgrave Macmillan.

Spears, L. (2010). Servant Leadership and Robert K. Greenleaf's Legacy. In D. Van Dierendonck & K. A. Patterson (Eds.), *Servant Leadership: Developments in Theory and Research* (pp. 11–24). New York, NY: Palgrave Macmillan.

Van Dierendonck, D., & Patterson, K. A. (Eds.). (2010). *Servant Leadership: Developments in Theory and Research*. New York, NY: Palgrave Macmillan.

Witherington, B. (2016). *New Testament Theology and Ethics* (Vol. 1). Downers Grove, IL: InterVarsity Press.

Wright, N. T. (2012). *After You Believe: Why Christian Character Matters*. New York, NY: HarperCollins Publishers.

# 4

# Servant Leadership in the Old Testament

There is much that can be learned from the Old Testament Scriptures concerning servant leadership and its application to real situations in diverse contexts. As the Scripture is examined in the search for the divine perspective on leadership, the goal is to answer the questions on servant leadership but further it is to ask the bigger question about biblical leadership. Is there a biblical construct or model for leadership? Is this model servant leadership or a more nuanced and critiqued model of servant leadership? What can be learned about leadership and organizations from a careful analysis of several texts of Scripture? The reality is though that all the relevant texts cannot be examined in this short study but several will be selected and examined using current methods of hermeneutics which fits under the category of qualitative analysis.

A word about method and the analytical process of Scripture or exegesis is in order at the beginning of this study. The first task of Biblical interpretation is called exegesis, which is the careful systematic study of Scripture to discover the original, intended meaning, to hear the original intent of the words as the original recipients would hear it (Fee & Stuart, 2014). This process is looking for authorial intent remembering that there is both a human and divine author. Hermeneutics then is the

© The Author(s) 2018
S. Crowther, *Biblical Servant Leadership*, Christian Faith Perspectives in Leadership and Business, https://doi.org/10.1007/978-3-319-89569-7_4

science of interpretation (Fee & Stuart, 2014). The question is how is this examination of Scripture done?

This process begins with careful and detailed observation. In this study, there will be a combination of related methods used for this exegetical analysis. One method is called the historical grammatical method. This method is concerned with context and direct meanings from the literal grammatical sense of the text. The issue of context includes many different kinds of contexts from literary to historical. Then there is the method of inductive Bible study that looks inductively at the text with asking questions of the text in the search for what is really there in the text. The final method and the default method used will be Socio-Rhetorical Interpretation. This approach invites detailed attention to the text itself by moving interactively into the world of the people who write the text and the present world and it is a combination of approaches aimed at showing the textures in the text (Robbins, 1996). It is not looking for multiple meanings in the text, but it is looking for issues and discoveries that are hidden from us since we are so far removed from the original audience. The specific ways of doing this type of analysis is divided into several categories each with their own emphases and definitions. These categories are inner texture, intertexture, social and cultural texture, ideological texture, and sacred texture (Robbins, 1996). These concepts will be discussed throughout this study as these methods are used in the process of interpretation. There is some overlap in these methods and this can help in this process of interpretation to see the nuances of the divine perspective from Scripture.

The final step in this analytical process is application. In the Western world, through the focus on pragmatism, the tendency is to rush to application. In reality, many read Scripture and apply it without bothering to stop along the path for a moment of interpretation. Interpretation is what does it say to the original audience, what is the authorial intent of this message. Then application is taking that clear message and appropriating it to the present context making allowance for cultural and contextual differences. Without this slow process of moving from observation to interpretation to application, Scripture can become just endorsement of our latest fads or an archaic self-help book. Scripture is more than this and it needs the time for careful analysis to be able to receive the message that is life changing from a divine perspective.

As the Old Testament is examined, there is a further interpretive problem. It is an Old Covenant that has been superseded by a new one. Should it be rejected as old or should it just be simply brought into the present ignoring the different covenants? Neither is a good answer. Others have tried these answers without good results. The Old Testament is revelatory. God's mind and purposes are really revealed in and through it. The Old Testament is provisional finding its ultimate interpretation and norm in the revelation of Jesus Christ and its appropriation by the New Testament. Therefore, the Old Testament is appropriated by means of Jesus as its ultimate fulfillment and normative interpretation. In interpretation of the Old Testament, the text needs to be carefully reviewed finding the message of timeless truths and then looking for ways that these texts are fulfilled in Christ and the New Covenant as their interpretive metric.

## Examples of Leaders in the Old Testament

### Genesis: Joseph

The classic story of a servant leader is the story of Joseph. The Old Testament shows his development from childhood through adulthood with several important stops along the way. He was sold into slavery but still managed to become a servant leader on different levels and in different contexts from prison to the palace of Egypt. Joseph is only one of three characters of the Bible in whom no sin is revealed, along with Jesus and Daniel he is presented as a flawless hero though this not imply a life without sin in Joseph, it is meant to compare the best of Joseph with the worst of his brothers (Bauchman, 2013). The story of Joseph begins in Genesis 37 and weaves itself through the rest of the book of Genesis through chapter 50. This larger-than-life hero begins as a misunderstood dreamer who has dreams that imply others will bow down to him, even his brothers and father. This is a classic story of jealousy as the brothers decide to kill him when there is opportunity and when they are a great distance from home since Jacob, the father, loved and protected Joseph. In the process of the plot to kill him, they decide instead to sell him to some traders as a slave in Genesis 37:28. They deceived their father Jacob convincing him that Joseph had been killed by a wild animal.

Joseph's life begins as a slave in Egypt. First, he begins as a servant to the captain in Pharaoh's army of Egypt (Genesis 37:36). He served the captain faithfully and was even promoted until the wife of the captain falsely accused him of improper advances against her and Joseph was thrown into prison as a result of this event (Genesis 39:11–20). Then in the prison he serves the prison keeper and even the other prisoners. He interprets two dreams for two important prisoners, who had been close to the king and these dreams come true but the cupbearer who was restored to the king forgot about Joseph (Genesis 40:6–8; 16–23). Joseph's suffering was not over. Yet, two years later, Pharaoh had a dream and this cupbearer remembered Joseph. This was a dream that impacted all of Egypt and none could interpret it, but Joseph interprets it with great detail and even with instructions on how to deal with the coming calamity, and Pharaoh appoints Joseph as second in Egypt to deal with this impending disaster (Genesis 41:37–41). What a sudden change! This was a long time in coming but it did come and in a way it came overnight, everything changed in one day. This promotion to a strategic position is an example of expansion as Joseph passed an integrity check which is a test to shape character, and it is often delayed as in the case of Joseph who passed the initial test in the situation with the wife of the captain (Clinton, 2012). At times, even the best of leaders are slow to be recognized, this is not necessarily from a wrong direction or a misstep by the person but simply part of the process as is seen here in Joseph.

The famine comes to all of the nations around Egypt as well as to Egypt. This drives the surrounding nations and tribes to Egypt to negotiate trade with Egypt since they were the only nation with the real vision of the future and then prepared for it under the leadership of Joseph. In this mixture of nations and tribes, Joseph's brothers return to him to buy food though they do not know that he is their brother (Genesis 42:7–8). He sells them food but tests them several times in the process as they return for more food from Genesis 42 to Genesis 44. When Joseph decides to reveal himself to his brothers, it shows some of the conflict inside of him. He had never given up on his father or even his brothers who betrayed him, here in this exalted position he served them and literally saved them from famine. Yet, he had been a faithful and good servant to

Egypt and Pharaoh. Would there be conflict in this revelation of himself and who would he choose to serve. In Genesis 45:1, he had everyone except his brothers leave the room and he made himself known to his brothers. "He wept so loudly that the Egyptians heard it, and the household of Pharaoh heard of it" (Genesis 45:2). As a result, Pharaoh received Joseph's family and they lived close to Joseph and were well provided for throughout the time of Joseph and the Pharaoh. Joseph led as a servant for the remainder of his life and he even saw the third generation of his sons as a legacy if his leadership and he made them promise to return his bones to the land of promise when they returned to Israel (Genesis 50:23–25).

In Joseph is found a servant leader first to his family but then to those around him wherever he found himself, including prison. Eventually, he became servant to Pharaoh and ultimately to his whole family again. There are two takeaways from the end of the story of Joseph: that of forgiveness and hope (Bauchman, 2013). Joseph rises to the occasion to forgive all of those who wronged him and does not become the victim of bitterness. There are two choices in suffering, especially when it is at the hands of other humans, bitterness which breeds revenge or perseverance which breeds character and hope. Paul says in Romans 5:3–4, "We exult in our tribulations, knowing that tribulation brings about perseverance; and perseverance, proven character; and proven character hope." Finding the place of joy and perseverance in the midst of the pressures of life breeds good character and hope. These are two of the qualities that are seen in Joseph. He seemed to always have the ability to see the future with hope even as a teenager. He saw the future in dreams, but he also saw the future in people—not only in his fellow prisoners but also in his brothers though they failed many times; he saw more in them and helped to bring that out in them for the good of all. His focus on testing and helping his brothers into the future brought benefit not only to them but to Joseph and even to the nations of Egypt and Israel. There is not a better picture in the Old Testament of servant leadership. However, here is seen some of the inside workings of servant leadership in character development in areas like integrity and forgiveness in overcoming self-focus. In addition, hope is also seen in Joseph not just for himself and his nation but also for his failing troubled brothers.

## Exodus 3 and 18: Moses

In some senses, Moses was a servant leader though he was in government service in leading the nation of Israel. He was a person of humility as well as a person who was able to effectively delegate to others. The concept of inner texture sets the context for this pericope in Exodus 3:1–15. The inner texture of a text resides in the features of the language, like word repetition and use of dialogue between two persons that sets the sections off from each other with a beginning, middle, and ending (Robbins, 1996). This concept divides this portion of Scripture into three sections giving insight into three qualities of leadership.

The first of the three scenes begins and ends focusing on Moses in verse 1 then in verse 4. The body of this section discusses the call of Moses in a narrational texture or format. The second section begins with a command from the Lord for Moses not to "come near here," in verse 5 and concludes in verse 10 with a directive from the Lord to "come now and I will send you." The body of this section is direct speech from God to Moses as the Lord continues to deepen the call to Moses as well as add this encounter of Moses with God. The third section begins with Moses asking God a question in verse 11, "Who am I that I should go?" This section and the pericope ends with God answering Moses' question in verse 15 declaring this is Who I am. The body here continues to deepen the call of Moses and further deepen the encounter between Moses and God while adding a third element of humility. This portion is an exchange of direct speech between God and Moses.

This pericope also has a repetitive and progressive texture in the midst of the narrational texture. The first section focuses on the repetition of Moses, the Lord, and the burning bush. The second section focuses on the repetition of Israel, God, and Egypt. While the third section focuses on Moses, name, and God. There is a progression here as the scene opens with narration concerning Moses and the Lord then transitions to directives given by the Lord to Moses concerning Israel and Egypt. But this does not conclude the pericope as the third scene moves to a much more personal encounter between Moses and God. The directives from God to Moses forced a personal encounter between God and Moses answering the question of who is God and who is Moses. This is a progressive encounter that ends with a revelation of God to Moses and to the reader as well (Table 4.1).

This whole pericope begins with the Lord calling to Moses out of obscurity and ends with the Lord revealing something personal and eternal to Moses of Himself. The story moves from the call of God to Moses that becomes deeply personal through Moses' encounter with God in this context revealing both the personal, powerful nature of God and the humility of Moses.

The story opens in the first section with Moses tending sheep close to the mountain of God. The Lord appears to him under the physical impression of a burning bush. The miraculous part is not the burning bush in a desert but the fact that it does not burn up. This peaks the interest of Moses. But as Moses approached the bush, the Lord called to him. This is the first indication of the call of Moses from the Lord. This call deepens throughout the story but it begins here as the Lord begins to speak to Moses out of obscurity in a surprising way from a surprising place. Jethro, his father-in-law, was a priest of El or Elohim, the only name known for

**Table 4.1** Repetitive and progressive texture of scenes of Exodus 3:1–15

| | | | | | | | |
|---|---|---|---|---|---|---|---|
| **Exodus 3:1–4 Initial call of Moses: scene one** | | | | | | | |
| 1 | Moses | | | God | | Mountain | |
| 2 | | Bush (3x) Fire (2x) | | | The Lord | | |
| 3 | Moses | Bush | | | | | |
| 4 | Moses (2x) | Bush | | God | The Lord | | |
| **Exodus 3:5–10 God encounters Moses: scene two** | | | | | | | |
| 6 | Moses | | | God (5x) | | | Do not come near |
| 7 | | Egypt | | | The Lord | | |
| 8 | | Egyptians | | | | | |
| 9 | | Egyptians | Israel | | | | |
| 10 | | Egypt | Israel | | | | Come now and I will send |
| **Exodus 3:11–15 Moses encounters God in humility: scene three** | | | | | | | |
| 11 | Moses | Egypt | Israel | God | | | Who am I |
| 12 | | Egypt | | God | | Mountain | |
| 13 | Moses | | Israel | God | Name (2x) | | |

God before this incident in Exodus 3. This only known name for God will change in this importnat encounter between God and Moses. God met with Moses in the process of life not in the performance of a religious duty.

This call was first of all from God, but it was also to a particular vocation or situation which involved leadership. Moses became a great leader but he was not only a spiritual leader he was also a governmental leader of Israel. One of the principles from this pericope is that leadership begins in the mind of God, as a gracious inclusion of humanity into the plans and purposes of God (Willimon, 2002). Leadership begins with a call from God that can come in the process of life to a vocation that is not necessarily religious in nature. There are spiritual truths in leadership and it begins with God and His call for an individual, but this is not restricted to religious vocations; Moses' call was not restricted in such a manner. These characteristics operated in Moses as a result of a spiritual occurrence. Social, cultural realities were important here but they were not the cause or source of this leadership that proceeded from Moses. On the most basic level of cause and motivation, it came from God in the form of calling from God to a mission or vision.

In the second section from verse 5 to verse 10, the concept of call continues in God speaking directly to Moses concerning the nature of his vocation and the particular situation into which Moses is being sent. God begins to encounter Moses with the reality of His presence at which initially Moses hides his face. In this encounter, God is the initiator and reveals His name to Moses while instructing him not to come near. In this encounter is a revelation of God and a revelation of God's design for Moses. In this direct speech, God shows that He has seen the affliction of Israel and wants Moses to go and lead them out of Egypt. This is a very specific leadership vocation from God. It begins with a call to come to God but it ends with a movement in relationship from "Do not come" to "Come now" and with a sending to fulfill this vocation of leadership. Leadership qualities of Moses proceed from Moses' connection to God, from his engagement with God. It is almost as if God goes out of His way to choose people who do not seem to have the qualities of good leaders, perhaps because God considers vocation a continuing aspect of creation (Willimon, 2002). It is this engagement with God that brings Moses to great leadership, not so much from what he knows as much as the change that occurs in his encounters with God. Calling from God leads to encounter with God that defines not only vocation but also begins to form the person for true leadership. One is not called first to some special work but to God, the key is devotion to nothing above God Himself (Guinness, 2003). Calling begins with encounter with God that changes the person and sends them into specific vocation. These are two essential foundations for leadership that are missed in the zeal to find the ingredients of a good leader. Biblical leadership starts in unseen realms with God and then moves to the internal life and experience of the person that is unique to that person but begins with call from God and encounter with God.

The third section begins with an adversative wherein Moses interjects into the soliloquy of the Lord. Once the revelation of God's design for Moses' vocation becomes apparent, Moses begins to speak. He asks a question of his identity and his ability to perform such an incredible task. Was this humility or the beginning of Moses' resistance to the declared purpose of God for him? It is likely here that the question is used in a humble, self-depreciating sense or is it the beginning of resistance; however, God's assurance in verse 12 that He will be with Moses, in a sense, accepts Moses' reaction as legitimate (Janzen, 2000). A third essential ingredient for leadership as seen in the life of Moses is humility.

However, Moses' encounter is not over with the Lord in this story of his call to leadership. After Moses' declaration of his inability, God says He will be with Moses. But Moses inquired further into the name of the Lord, the one who was sending him. God had already told him He was the God of their fathers, the God of Abraham, Isaac, and Jacob, but Moses presses for something more. Interestingly, God's response is first to Moses himself and only then to the matter of what name he should bring to the Israelites, suggesting here that Moses is asking his own searching question, *who are you really* (Janzen, 2000)? This is a personal encounter between Moses and God with far-reaching implications. Would Moses embrace this call to go to Israel? First, he had to settle who he was but this could only be settled in light of who God was. This is one of the most discussed passages of the whole Old Testament, and it plays on the relationship, between grammar and sound, between the Hebrew word "to be" and the divine name Yahweh (Janzen, 2000). Few verses in the Old Testament cause such heated controversy and diverse interpretations; how does the giving of the name validate Moses' claim to divine revelation and how is this "I am who I am" to be translated (Childs, 1975). Childs goes on to propose several possible solutions but none that are final and definitive. A solution is to take seriously Israel's tradition and emphasize the newness of the name to Moses (Childs, 1975). Janzen (2000) instead proposes translating the phrase into the future tense to show the dynamic character of God.

However, neither of these theological constructs takes into account the true nature of this encounter between Moses and God. This encounter first was personal before it was directed at Israel. This answer proceeded from Moses' acknowledgement of his inability to fulfill this call to go to Egypt. In the process of Socio-Rhetorical Interpretation, sacred texture is seeking the divine in the text and finding insights into the nature of the relationship between human and divine (Robbins, 1996). In the sacred texture of this pericope, there are answers to some of these types of questions about the relationship between the individual and God. There are times that Scripture is viewed from an outsider perspective; the events are watched from the perspective of by-standers to consider the ramifications later. This is one of those times, which occurs frequently in the life of Moses. In this encounter, God encountered Moses in a new way, no longer as the God of Abraham but as the God of "I am." In essence the same way that he encountered Abraham not as the God of the past but of the God of the present. Also He did not come as the God of someone else but as the God, the imminent God of that person. So God came to Moses as the God of I am, He came as the God of Moses not the God of the fathers but the God who is present in encounter with you, Moses. This is seen here from the outside so we miss the deeply personal nature of this encounter. Then this offer of the God of the fathers becoming the God of Israel was to be made to Israel. This is God's name forever; it is still His name to each person who answers His call. We have missed the point by trying to discover His name, though that is valuable, and not realizing the purpose of this moment was encounter; yes it was a new name but a name that calls for encounter with God. This is who He is.

Up to this point God was known as El with some hyphenated description like *El-Elyon* or as *Elohim*. The name *Yahweh* is introduced in this text as a name so far unknown to Moses and Israel, although it refers to the same God that the fathers had worshipped, and in revealing a new name He introduces a new role, that of Savior/Liberator/Redeemer (Janzen, 2000). This encounter deeply changes Moses and would have far-reaching implications for Israel. God now wanted to come up close to Israel both symbolically and relationally. The drama of this new Name and new role is played out in the wilderness over the next 40 years and as Israel settles into her own land. This was a pivotal moment for Moses, for Israel, and for redemptive history. But if that is all we see we have missed the point of God being "I am" to us. The sacred texture of this text opens the text to us beyond theology to personal experience. This encounter changed Moses' life, perspective, and leadership. This was an internal change as his life was deeply influenced by the presence of God which engendered more encounters with God, a deeper sense of call, and a profound humility.

Moses is continuing in ministry in Exodus 18:17–24. Jethro, his father-in-law and a Midianite priest, gives him counsel, which Moses receives and implements. Jethro gives Moses three specific instructions that are relevant to the discussion of leadership. First, Moses you lead out of your encounter with God. You go to God to represent the people, pray for them, and bring the disputes to God; you help them get answers from God. Not only are you to mediate for them but also take the words God has given you and teach the people the concepts of the Lord and the ramifications of those concepts for their lives and their work. This proceeds from Moses' initial and ongoing encounters with the Lord.

Second, Moses is instructed to select individuals and make them leaders over certain groupings of people. Moses was to let them take his place of ministry and leadership to the people; only the major disputes would come to Moses. This must proceed from the humility in Moses to release this kind of power and authority to thousands of other people. This is an example of effective delegation and promotion of team ministry. However, these two constructs for leadership cannot simply be done under constraint; there must be an internal drive to give momentum to this leadership paradigm. This drive comes from humility to have confidence in others as well as a realistic assessment of self.

Third, Moses is instructed to do these things so it would be easier for him and the other leaders would bear the burden of leadership with him.

Moses chose able men, men who stand in awe of God and who have integrity. These men were to be placed in leadership. Choosing other leaders is an important aspect of leadership particularly when there is a divine mission or vision to be fulfilled. Moses brought thousands of people into leadership at this time and helped them find and fulfill the call of God for their lives. Part of fulfilling calling from God is to help others find and fulfill their call together with you. Moses led out of his calling, which brought a sense of destiny to the Israelites and made him an effective leader in bringing others into calling and leadership. Moses led out of his encounter with God. This encounter deeply changed his life and he was able to connect with God for other people, to help them connect with God, and to teach others about knowing and following God and His principles. Moses led from a position of authority with humility and as a result he was able to appoint others to come with him into leadership.

In Moses are seen several issues of servant leadership. The contemporary theory of servant leadership as discussed by contemporary leadership theorists includes humility as one of the attributes in this form of leadership. Servant leadership includes seven virtuous constructs of which one is humility, while some consider humility a weakness, it is a virtue of not over-valuing oneself and respects the worth of others (Patterson, 2003). Humility is a virtue that becomes apparent in the life of Moses in the midst of this initial call experience and continues to be a characteristic of his leadership throughout his ministry. However, it is clear that humility was not a predominant characteristic in the earlier life of Moses when he killed the Egyptian taking it upon himself to help Israel. This was evidence of pride not humility. Something had changed by this time and this change was in Moses. Humility can be an acquired trait and it is extremely important for leadership as seen in the life of Moses. For godly leaders, positional authority and the disposition of humility should not be mutually exclusive; the two may coexist within the character of the leader and this goes to the heart of the uniqueness of Christian leadership (Ayers, 2006). Biblical leadership includes humility which can be a learned virtue yet is at the heart of the issue of leadership. Many activities flow from this humility that produces good leadership, activities such as consideration, moderation, considering others, and a desire to listen to others. These type of leaders realize that they do not have all of the answers and the greatest gift that a leader can give a follower is the gift of self and this comes from humility (Patterson, 2003). Humility is a realistic self-assessment that does not produce self-rejection but instead produces reliance upon others with a confidence in giving self to others.

In addition, Moses is very effective at empowering others here on a large scale with huge implications for Israel. Moses is seen as called into service of the Lord but he is to serve the people. He serves for the most part for the rest of his life. Nevertheless, there are some issues that fall outside the normal parameters of servant leadership. These would include the issues of calling and encounter with God. Are these part of servant leadership or are these only components that can fit into Christian leadership? First, finding purpose is an issue for all and not just for Christians. This could become a further area of study to nuance servant leadership. However, encounter with God in the way that we see here with Moses is a uniquely Christian and Jewish concept. Where would this fit into the study of leadership? Possibly, it would fit in the area of uniquely Christian leadership.

## Esther 4–5: Esther

Esther becomes a servant to the people of Israel and even a foreign Gentile nation based upon a position that she did not seek. In this story is seen the instruction of Mordecai in teaching her to lead. Esther demonstrates effective leadership in a difficult situation, but she does so by not placing herself in the limelight, and further she is marginalized in a forced marriage and is asked to lead where she has no power at the risk of her life (Akinyele, 2009). In Esther 4, her uncle comes to ask her to risk her life to serve the people of Israel and save them from extinction. Then in Esther 4:16, she affirms that she will go in to ask the king for a favor at the risk of her life. She thwarts the evil plans of Haman, who wants to destroy the people of Israel. However, the intrigue is in how she brings this deliverance. She risks her life to go in to the king unannounced, to ask the king and Haman to come to a banquet which they do, according to Esther 5:5. When they attend the banquet, she simply invites them to a new banquet, "So my request is that if I have found favor in the sight of the king and if it pleases the king to grant my petition … may the king and Haman come to the banquet that I will prepare for them" (Esther 5:7–8). She is not pressing them but she is serving them and Haman actually thinks this is a good sign for his rise to power. However, there is a secret that neither the king nor Haman know about this situation. The Queen is an Israelite!

At the next banquet, the Queen reveals what is happening and how Haman wants to destroy her people, the Jews. The king is enraged and Haman is executed (Esther 7:7–9). Then Esther and even her uncle are rewarded. The most intriguing statement among many in the book of Esther is this statement in Esther 4:14 when Mordecai, Esther's uncle, says to her, "Who knows whether you have not attained royalty for such a time as this?" This was an issue of calling and destiny over the life of Esther, who rose from obscurity in bizarre circumstances to become queen in the most powerful land of the time to save Israel. This was not circumstance; this was with purpose, divine purpose. She develops as a servant in a humble household with no advantages yet becomes a person of advantage and in this place was pressed into leadership. Yet, she chose to lead as a servant. She served with humility and altruism, considering others before herself in risking her life to save the many Israelites of her time in her nation.

## Instructions for Leaders in the Old Testament

There are instructions in the Old Testament text for learning to serve and lead in both positive aspects as in the instructions to Joshua and in a negative sense in the counsel given to Rehoboam, the son of Solomon. Joshua is told to be strong and courageous several times at the beginning of his ministry in Joshua 1. Does courage fit into a model for leadership? Aristotle considered courage as one of the four virtues for human flourishing. This is not normally considered as part of servant leadership yet this brings a need for this discussion to the forefront.

Then Rehoboam is Solomon's son and a new King in 2 Chronicles 10. The leaders of Israel come to him to discuss his coming rule over them. Rehoboam was told by the elders to be kind and the people would serve him. He was told to become their servant but he refused and came as a domineering leader. This split the Kingdom of Israel into two kingdoms, a breech that is not easily repaired. Here, servant leadership is seen as the only answer to this dilemma yet when refused it brought disaster.

# God as the Model Leader in the Old Testament

However, the Old Testament provides the best example of a servant leader in that God is the ultimate leader and His leadership sets the example for others. He is seen as the shepherd with a heart for people (Psalm 23:1) and who is angered when the human shepherd leaders treat their followers with oppression based in selfish goals (Ezekiel 34:1–24 and Jeremiah 23:1–4). These last two pericopes of rebuke to the shepherds will be examined in detail later in this study. Here is seen the essence of instruction for servant leaders as well in the rebukes given to these leaders of Israel in the context of the Old Testament.

# Pictures of Leaders in the Old Testament

## Shepherd: Kings, Priests, Elders

There are some overall pictures of servant leadership in different types of leaders and the way that God views them and their function. In the Old Testament, kings, priests, elders, and other government leaders are called shepherds. This is the major word picture in the Old Testament for leadership. However, this picture is nuanced by the instructions that the Lord gives to these shepherds of His people. The concept of shepherd as applied to leaders among God's people is traditional and is applied to God and God's leadership style as well as to human leaders in the Old Testament (Witherington, 2007). This is a metaphor for leadership that is filled with significance for those who lived in this age of the Old Testament. One of the primary metaphors which biblical authors use for leadership is that of shepherd, and God has a divine preference for human agency and He chooses regularly to engage humans in the tasks of leadership

(Laniak, 2006). This preference for human agency shows up through the pages of the Old Testament as God chooses leaders, instructs leaders, and even rebukes leaders in His development of the people of God.

However, another major word used for leader in the Old Testament is that of "servant." The language of servanthood is pervasive through the Old Testament with 16 different words for servanthood, and the concept of servanthood embraces the whole range of Old Testament leaders (Davidson, 2014). The prophets and even kings and priests as well as other people in general are seen as servants and leaders. In addition, there is a picture here of a suffering servant who turns out to be the Messiah in a prophetic passage of the ministry of Jesus. Then it is noteworthy how many women provide leadership while using explicit language of servanthood in describing their role; though most of these women did not hold official positions, they still led (Davidson, 2014). There is an abundance of evidence in the Old Testament for servants who are leaders in many different contexts providing a foundation for understanding leadership from a biblical perspective. In this search for biblical servant leadership, insights are gained for leadership through these direct and indirect messages to leaders as His shepherds and servants.

## Suffering Servant: Isaiah 52–53

In Isaiah 52 and 53, there is a portrayal of the Messiah as the suffering servant that is picked up and developed later in the New Testament. The description of the Suffering Servant as an ideal leader connects to the prophetic hope of a future perfect king on the Davidic throne (Peterson, 2014). This picture begins in Isaiah 52 with the servant acting wisely and being exalted in the context of kings. Yet in chapter 53, he is described as growing up with no apparent beauty or majesty, and he was despised and rejected (Isaiah 53:2–3). This prophetic word speaks at length in a prophetic sense of the coming ministry of Jesus. He was a servant of the Lord and he served the people by bearing their iniquities, sins, and infirmities. This passage is full of conflict and contrasts. There will be anguish in His soul yet he will be satisfied (Isaiah 53:11). He will make many to be accounted as righteous through his service, and he bore the sin of many yet he still makes intercession for the transgressors (Isaiah 53:8). Here is seen the ultimate in paradox in serving those who are underserving. This Messiah becomes the ultimate servant leader, literally laying down His life for those who are underserving. This is the crux of the gospel and yet the ultimate in servant leadership, a servant leader who dies to redeem followers and then intercedes for not only followers but the persecutors as well.

## Levites

The Levites were to serve the people, the priests, and the Lord at the tabernacle and later at the temple in some very menial tasks yet later we find them as the teachers and leaders of the people. Both Moses and Aaron, the early leaders in Israel, were from the tribe of Levi. Though the Levites are seen in Exodus and Leviticus, their function is introduced in Numbers 1:47–54. They are to carry the tabernacle and the furnishings and to camp around it. They are servants for the tabernacle and to the people. They were also not counted or given an inheritance like the other tribes. Their inheritance was the Lord and their work. Then the ministry of the Levites is seen again in Numbers 8:5–22. In verses 14–15, the Lord says the Levites are His and they have a special purpose in serving Him. The Levites are to go in and serve the tent of meeting. They were the servants to do the physical work of setting up the tabernacle and moving it when the camp moved, and they were to keep all of the physical elements in order.

However, during the time of David in 1 Chronicles 15:22–28, many generations later the Levites are appointed by David to lead worship to the Lord with different instruments and singing. Then when the tabernacle becomes a permanent temple under Solomon, this ministry of leading worship continues. Even under the later King Hezekiah, the Levites led worship. Nevertheless, the temple was destroyed under the conquest and rule of the Babylonians. In the restoration, it was Ezra, the priest, along with the Levites who taught all of the people the word of God and restored the temple. In the Old Testament, the Levites begin as physical servants to the tabernacle, but through faithfulness they become worship leaders, leaders who teach and even leaders who lead national restoration. In the Levites servanthood is seen as a place of growth and influence in leadership that grows in the doing of service to others.

# The Prophets as Servants: Jeremiah, Ezekiel, Elijah

The prophets are servants to the Lord and they served the people as well and even kings though many times their service was rejected. The leadership role of prophet is intimately connected with the leadership role of the king in the ancient world and these prophets understood their role as a calling more than an occupation (Stevens, 2012). The prophets were called by God to speak to and serve the king and the people by speaking the word of God to them. There are several texts in the Old Testament that give important insights for servant leadership in these contexts. In Psalms 23:1 and in Isaiah 40:11, the Lord Himself is seen as a shepherd leader who gently guides and carries the flock or the lambs and this flock shall not be in need. It is a picture of leadership that is played out in other sections and other prophets and even in kings, as shall be seen in Saul and David. Then Isaiah proceeds in Isaiah 42 to talk about the Servant of the Lord. This points toward the Messiah yet is still significant that kings and prophets were called servants and in this context to rule is to serve and suffer and to lead is both to suffer and be a sacrificial lamb (Laniak, 2006). Do all leaders become sacrificial and/or do they suffer? This is an important line of thought to pursue in this study.

Leaders during the days of the prophets were admonished to exercise justice and compassion while humbling themselves before God, and these prophetic messages provide fundamental and divinely revealed principles of leadership for all ages (Peterson, 2014). These prophets provided direction for these shepherd leaders often through rebuke. Jeremiah prophesied that it was the fault of leadership in Israel for the condition of Israel in causing the Babylonian captivity and the prophet issues woes or rebukes to these leaders or shepherds of Israel. The message of Jeremiah to the leaders is a prophetic solution for Israel though it is not just a return to theocracy but it is a return to the Davidic times of a return of the Shepherd of Israel (Laniak, 2006). In other words, there was a new time coming with a return to this shepherd leadership that is endorsed in Isaiah, Jeremiah, and Ezekiel. Ezekiel not only criticizes the rulers but also blames them for the imminent apocalypse, correcting them through metaphor and direct address with the most developed leadership expose found in chapter 34 to the shepherds (Laniak, 2006). First, the leaders are rebuked for how they have not shepherded the sheep then the Lord says He will become the shepherd of the people. There are many instructions as to what the leaders did incorrectly that stands as clear instruction in what shepherd leaders should do or become. This list will be detailed later in the study in the failure of leaders in the Old Testament. In this search of the Old Testament, both Servant and Shepherd motifs come to the surface as images for leadership. Are these two compatible or do they bring different nuances to the concept of leadership or even servant leadership itself? As this study proceeds, this will be a question that is discussed for its connection to contemporary issues of servant leadership.

## The Texts of Servant Leadership in the Old Testament

### 2 Sam. 17:27–29; 19:31–40; 1 Kings 2:7—Barzillai

Some of these texts show examples of good servant leaders like Barzillai who was so good at serving that most people did not even know who he was or what he did, but he came and served King David at a very vulnerable time in the king's life. Barzillai is introduced as part of a group in 2 Samuel 17 who brings supplies to David to help him as he is on the run from Absalom, David's son, who had taken the kingdom from David. Then Barzillai is seen again in the camp of David as David returns victorious to Jerusalem; here there is an extended dialogue between the two men in 2 Samuel 19:31–33. In these verses, David invites Barzillai to return with him as a victor and to participate in all of the rewards of a retuned kingdom with all of its wealth and splendor. Barzillai refuses because he is old and it would not do him any good to receive these kinds of rich rewards. Then he refers to himself three times as David's servant. Then they blessed one another and parted ways. Here was a true servant who served David in his time of need yet needed and wanted no reward; he simply wanted to be considered David's servant. Even later as David was dying in 1 Kings 2:7, he remembered Barzillai and mentioned him for blessing to his son Solomon. What profound impact this one unknown servant had on the king and the blessing from this service passed down to the next generation.

## 1 Kings 3: Solomon

Consider Solomon who when given the opportunity by the Lord for wealth and power took wisdom to rule instead. In 1 Kings 3, Solomon is offering sacrifices to God at the beginning of his rule of Israel. He offered a thousand burnt offerings. At the end of the offerings, God comes to Solomon in a dream and tells him to ask for whatever he wants. This is quite open ended. In his answer, he calls both David and himself servants. Then he calls himself a servant three separate times in his answer. However, what he asks for is wisdom or a discerning heart to govern the people. He wants to be able to know right from wrong in leading the people. Solomon's desire is to embody the Hebrew concept of wisdom with practical application for the benefit of the people (Wibberding, 2014). Here is a servant's heart, his first concern is to know how to do well and lead well with people in his charge. The Lord is so happy with this answer that He also gives Solomon wealth and fame which he did not request. The Lord's answer here provides insight for leadership issues. The normal answer according to the Lord would have been to request wealth or victory over enemies. However, He indicated that Solomon did not ask for blessings for himself; therefore, God was going to bless him beyond his request to be able to serve well. What did Solomon want? He wanted wisdom to serve the people, he wanted to discern right from wrong, and he wanted ethical leadership ability. Ethical leadership may be implied in servant leadership but here is a call to pay attention to this issue as an extension or nuance for servant leadership. Then when servant leadership is pursued, does it bring blessings in other areas that are personal? It did for Solomon; is this true with others as well?

## Nehemiah

The most powerful picture is that of Nehemiah, a household servant who changed the world by serving the people of Israel in rebuilding Jerusalem. Nehemiah was a slave in service of the king but he desired to go to Jerusalem where he went and as a servant he became a leader of leaders and formed teams to accomplish the task of rebuilding the city walls

(Gane, 2014). Here is a man who wept over the broken condition of Jerusalem as he was living in a foreign Gentile kingdom in Nehemiah chapter 1. He then prayed and he appealed to the Lord calling Israel God's servants and referring to himself and Moses as God's servant. He saw himself as the servant of the Lord. Then he served the Lord by serving the people of Jerusalem by leading them in the rebuilding of the wall around Jerusalem. In this prayer, he appealed to God that the Lord would give him favor with the king and the king granted his desire to go to Jerusalem and rebuild its ruins. Nehemiah then rebuilt the wall through using teams and delegating authority or empowering others to lead their teams in the rebuilding project. He led with prayer and encouragement and the people had a mind to work (Nehemiah 4:6). They worked with all of their heart to rebuild this wall around Jerusalem that had fallen. In the midst of the building of the wall, he discovered that the poor in the area were being oppressed by the wealthier Israelites. He found that the wealthy were exacting usury from the poor, even taking property from them to settle debts and he made them reverse this practice. They said, "We will restore these and require nothing from them. We will do as you say" (Nehemiah 5:12). Even the community and society around Nehemiah benefitted from his leadership and in this way he was operating altruistically.

Nehemiah restored the Levites, the singers, and the worshippers in Jerusalem and restored order in Jerusalem. In this restoration, Ezra the priest steps forward and reads from the text of the Scripture for the first time in many years. The people of Jerusalem celebrated for seven days followed by repentance and a time of bringing in new people into the city along with many more Priests and Levites. In his final reforms, Nehemiah restored the offerings and the tithe to support the Priests and the Levites and he purifies the priesthood and the Levites while assigning them their duties. In this activity is seen that Nehemiah sees himself as the servant of the Lord and yet He serves the people in several different ways for their benefit. He helps restore the wall through team leadership and participation. He altruistically looks out for others, even the poor who are being oppressed around him. Then, finally, he restores worship, the priesthood, and the word of God to Jerusalem so that they can be servants of God as well.

# 1 Samuel: David and Saul

There is a contrast between two Kings in David and Saul in showing the difference between autocratic and servant leadership. Nevertheless, David also exhibited other forms of leadership, like charismatic leadership. Here is a classic tale of two kings in a struggle for power, and while one has all of the advantages, the other has godly responses.

According to 1 Samuel 9–13, Saul's ascent came in stages wherein Saul was anointed by Samuel to be king, then the two met later on the road and finally when Saul was singled out by lot in the tribe of Benjamin; yet in all of this, Saul's modesty was shown as he hid behind the baggage when Samuel tried to introduce him (Lasor, Hubbard, & Bush, 1996). Was this humility in the beginning of the rule of Saul? Time will tell that it was not humility, or if there was humility here, it was not cultivated. Kings in Israel, once they became Kings, were to write out the law or the Pentateuch and were instructed in it not to exalt themselves above their countrymen and so they would not turn aside from the commandment of God (Deuteronomy 17:19–20). Saul had the humble beginnings and modesty and at least some direction from the law of God in not exalting himself even as the king. Yet as king, he continued to focus on self and exalting himself to his own detriment. This is seen from the beginning of his rule in 1 Samuel 13:2 when he chose men for himself, and when the battle began with the Philistines, it was Jonathan who won the first victory and yet Saul claimed it (1 Samuel 13:3–4). It gets worse when Saul makes a demand on the men and Jonathan unknowingly breaks it and then Saul tries to have Jonathan killed even though Jonathan had just led the troops to victory (1 Samuel 14:45). However, this flaw becomes even more evident when David enters the picture.

David kills the giant and becomes Saul's son-in-law in 1 Samuel 17 and 18 but it is of note in the final verse (vs. 30) of chapter 18 that David behaved more wisely than the other servants of Saul, so much so that his name was highly esteemed. David's fame was so widespread that even foreign kings heard the words of the song about David, "Saul had slain his thousands, and David his ten thousands" (1 Samuel 21:11). This did not sit well with Saul who from that time on began to try to kill David; he tried until his own death in battle years later. It is not the one who starts well who finishes a winning race; it is he who finishes well. It appears that Saul had opportunity to do well but he did not finish well. What happened? Pride, self-focus, and self-exaltation: the very issue he was warned against in becoming king became his downfall.

David takes a similar route to becoming king. He is anointed by the same prophet Samuel in 1 Samuel 16:10–13 where it is also seen that David's beginnings were so modest that even his own father did not consider him to be a candidate for king. He does immediately begin rule as king much in the same way that Saul began. David becomes a mighty warrior who gains fame for his valor to his own detriment in the design of Saul to kill him. David fled from Saul. Yet David had two unique chances to kill Saul and rid himself of his royal persecutor, once while Saul was alone in a cave (1 Samuel 24:2–9) and once when Saul was asleep (1 Samuel 26:6–16) but he did not kill him since Saul was the Lord's anointed. In both instances, Saul relented for a short time but returned soon enough to try to kill David. Ultimately in 1 Samuel 31:4, Saul dies and David slowly becomes king, though he deeply laments the death of Saul in 2 Samuel 1.

David becomes a great king in Israel through some turmoil but not of his doings. He restores a tabernacle for worship, he restores lands to Israel and even expands it, he writes many psalms as a worship leader, yet he also fails in the issues of adultery and murder surrounding the issue of his wife to be, Bathsheba. However, what kind of leader was he for Israel? David was a shepherd king. When all of the rulers of Israel came together to make David king, they said that previously when Saul was king David was the one who led us out and in and the Lord said to you, "you will shepherd my people Israel and you will be a ruler over Israel" (2 Samuel 5:2). There are two contrasting stories in David's rule: one of disobedience in the middle of his rule and another of hope and light and the end of his rule.

David committed adultery with Bathsheba and commanded the murder of her husband Uriah, one of his inner circle in 2 Samuel 11. He appears to get away with it but a prophet, Nathan, comes to him before the child is born and uncovers his sin with a story of a poor shepherd and designates David as the oppressor in the story. The prophet revealed how far David had fallen from being the shepherd of God's people and rather than protecting them on the battlefield he was at home sacrificing them for his own pleasure (Laniak, 2006). He failed as a shepherd; his job as a shepherd was to protect them, to consider them instead of moving into self-exaltation as Saul had done. Nevertheless, toward the end of his rule, David is seen again as a shepherd pleading for the people under a plague; in 2 Samuel 24:17, he appealed for the people since they were just sheep and the fault was his for this plague.

David was a great king but he still had flaws. He is a hero in spots but then in some areas he is the oppressor. It is significant that God does not let him get away with these flaws and he pays dearly for them but he continues to rule and to serve the Lord unlike Saul who was destroyed by his pride and bitterness against David. The testimony of the Lord is that David is a man after his own heart and this is twice repeated—once in 1 Samuel 13:14 and then in the New Testament in Acts 13:22. This does not mean he was perfect, but his heart was to do right even though through self-exaltation and self-focus he lost his way. However, he found strength to come back. His strength was in his worship and his deep connection to the Lord through which he was able to struggle back to effective leadership. The difference in his leadership from good to bad and back to good had several qualities. The first was he was to be a shepherd, to consider and care for the people as sheep before himself. The second was, as Saul, he would have known the law for kings not to exalt themselves above their countrymen, and, third, not turn aside from the law of God. Saul violated all three of these on a regular basis and David deeply violated the three on the issue of Bathsheba. David returned to become a great king while Saul was defeated and not honored by many except for David, the new king. The difference is David lived a life of humility and consideration for others until he was tempted and he fell into the pit of self-destruction. However, he repented and returned to do the hard work of serving others in spite of his past. Saul fell in the same pit but never returned. In this shepherd leadership, there are found three important attributes. Consideration and care for people before self is paramount with a second being not exalting self above peers and to be careful to follow the Lord. These first two qualities can be found in servant leadership as well, with the third found in Christian servant leadership.

# The Failure of Leadership in the Old Testament

The Old Testament gives several examples of failure in leadership and this failure repeatedly came through pride and self-focus in the leader. These examples are seen in the different sections of the Old Testament, with some leaders more faithful and successful than others but still with failures. It is important to see these failures not just as failures but instead as instructive for effective, good, and godly leadership.

## Judges: Samson, Gideon

Samson and Gideon both were called by God to be judges or leaders of Israel and they both failed but one succeeded first and failed in his legacy, whereas the other one failed from the beginning of his ministry. The theme of the book of Judges is that during this time everyone did what was right in their own eyes, but God would intervene by sending leaders from diverse corners of Israel to lead Israel out of oppression and to bring them back to a focus on serving the Lord. However, even the judges that were considered good leaders, like Gideon and Samson, marred their actions with wrong behavior like idolatry and even immorality (Moskala, 2014). The time of the judges is a good example of the failure of leadership in the Old Testament.

Gideon is an example of a leader who begins well yet the legacy he left for Israel brought disaster and destruction. In chapter 6 of Judges, Gideon is approached by an angel. Gideon responded to this call to deliver Israel from the Midianites with great humility and caution much like Moses before him. He needed to be convinced but once convinced he obeys the Lord's explicit instructions to reduce his army to 300 to face the thousands in the Midian army. Through divine strategy and intervention Gideon wins the day. Then Gideon is found in a dangerous place in Judges 8:23–28 wherein the people ask Gideon to rule over them. He answers well in saying neither he nor his children will rule over them. However, this is where the trouble begins. He wanted some of the spoils of gold from the Midianites and they gladly gave it to him. Then he formed an ephod from it; this was a priestly garment breastplate made of gold. The High Priest in the tabernacle was to wear one but these are not the same. This one made by Gideon was worshipped and the people committed immorality in their worship of it. However, they had 40 years of rest from their enemies in this idolatrous state. After Gideon's death, one of the sons killed most of the other 70 sons in a grab for power. This son of Gideon, Abimilech, ruled over Israel for three years of turmoil and died in a battle when a woman threw a millstone from a tower. Gideon was a man of humility and obedience to the Lord but in the end greed for power overcame him and his children. His legacy was one of disaster and turmoil. Great leaders are leaders who develop greatness in their organization past their present leadership era (Collins, 2001). Servant leaders produce other servant leaders. Gideon began as a servant leader to the Lord and to the people but along the way he lost this commitment in leadership by his attraction to self-exaltation and greed, which became his leadership legacy.

Samson begins with humble beginnings. He is listed as one of the men of old who gained approval by faith in Hebrews 11:32. He was considered a great leader of the faith yet he had some major issues that hindered his leadership along the way. Scripture gives us a very human picture of these leaders in both Old and New Testaments as lessons for the contemporary leader. This story of Samson certainly illustrates no New Testament ethic in that he was selfish and had no control of his passions, but there were some aspects that could be viewed positively as well (Lasor et al., 1996). Samson was clearly a flawed leader. He begins well in working against the Philistines who are oppressing Israel in Judges 14 and 15. However, he quickly falls into immorality in a forbidden relationship in Judges 16. He is deceived through his own blinded lust and captured by the Philistines and they physically blind him (Judges 16:20–21). Over his time as a prisoner, his strength and relationship with the Lord is restored. In a final act that takes his own life, he destroys many of the lords of the Philistines (Judges 16:28–30). This is not the destruction of the Philistines but it is a victory for Israel. This is similar to a contemporary story in the Star Wars saga. Young Anakin Skywalker fights against the dark side but enters into a forbidden relationship in the process. This time it is not the woman who deceives him through but his own lust for power through his distorted relationship with the emperor. Once deceived he is defeated and becomes the part machine Darth Vader. However, in the end, he participates in the destruction of this dark oppressive empire through a major victory on the battle star; though it does not end the empire, it does end many of their leaders. Samson is a warning to contemporary leaders. It is a warning to learn early to overcome self-exaltation and self-focus issues in the life and leadership development process. It is also a warning to be careful in starting well, not to be led off the path through pride and a focus on self, instead learning to have an increased focus on others and on calling. The judges warn us about the secret power of internal issues that can destroy a leader. These internal issues show up in the form of greed and lust but they begin with a focus on self that can increase with success.

## Prophets: Elisha's Servant

Here is Elisha, one of the greatest prophets of Israel, yet his servant failed the same test for leadership that Elisha had passed many years before him. Elisha was found by Elijah to become his servant shortly after Elijah had struggled with the Lord in the cave experience. The story is found at the end of 1 Kings 19 wherein Elijah throws his mantle over Elisha as an act of anointing him as prophet in his own place. Then 1 Kings 19:21 reveals the function of Elisha, "Then he arose and followed Elijah and ministered to him." He became his servant and he did it so well that he indeed becomes prophet in Elijah's place in 2 Kings 2:13–14. However, Elisha as the prophet has a servant as well and in 2 Kings 5 the captain of a foreign army comes for healing to Elisha. Elisha brings healing to him and the captain wants to reward Elisha but he rejects any reward. However, later the servant of Elisha, Gehazi, is found deceiving the captain to receive this reward for himself in 1 Kings 5:22–23. However, by the end of chapter 5, Gehazi is struck with leprosy and there is no one who follows Elisha to become prophet in his place. This is a tragedy not only for Elisha and the prophets; it is a tragedy for Israel. What was the problem? Gehazi chose not to serve as the path to leadership. Notice that even when Elijah and

Elisha were prophets, they had a heart for the people of Israel and served them in difficult circumstances. This call to leadership could not be done in any other way. Servant leadership is not only an effective way of leadership, but it is also an effective path to growth in leadership.

## Shepherds Who Failed Jeremiah 23, Ezekiel 34

The Lord gives two separate rebukes to failed shepherds and why they failed which gives instruction for shepherd leaders to follow in how to be good leaders. These rebukes come from two prophets during the early part of the exile of Judah in Babylon. While in the captivity, Jeremiah was still in the land of Judah and the other prophet Ezekiel was in the land of captivity, Babylon, yet they both spoke directly to the people and leaders of Israel.

In Jeremiah 23:1–4, Jeremiah rebukes the shepherds of Israel, not the natural shepherds but the leaders under the metaphor of sheep and shepherd. This is a climax to Jeremiah's condemnation of the last of several self-centered kings and this is a final woe on Judah's shepherds (Laniak, 2006). There is a thick inner texture here with repetitive, progressive, and open-middle-closing texture built upon a chiasm structure. The repetitive texture focuses on the word "shepherd" that is used four times in this short pericope while there are other words that are used twice, but these are used in almost mirror image ways in repetitive contrasts between how the shepherds have been tending and how God will tend his sheep. There is an open-middle-closing structure that forms a chiasm with an emphasis on the middle of this chiasm. The first half of the chiasm in two stanza's focuses on the shepherd's failure in leadership. The center focuses on what the Lord is going to do to them in an ironic twist. Then the second half focuses on what the Lord is going to do in providing leadership for his people.

> a. Woe to the shepherds who are destroying and scattering the sheep of my pasture
> b. You have scattered my flock and driven them away and have not attended to them
> c. I am about to attend to you for the evil of your deeds

b`. I myself will gather the remnant of my flock out of all the countries I have driven them and bring them back to their pasture and they will be fruitful and multiply

a`. I will also raise up shepherds over them and they will tend them and they will not be afraid any longer, nor be terrified, nor will any be missing (Jeremiah 23:1–4)

In addition, each section has a statement that this is a declaration of the Lord, four times in these four verses. His message to the bad leaders is that I am about to pay attention to you for the way that you did tend to and pay attention to my people. This would be an intensely terrifying word for any leader to hear.

The progressive texture is found in the progress of the narrative that goes from the rebuke for what the shepherds have done to the declaration of judgment as found in the middle of this tight declaration. Finally, it moves on to the resolution of God providing good shepherds. These good shepherds will provide the opposite of the evil ones. Then at the end there is a progressive list of how the people will respond to this leadership that will bring healing. They will no longer be afraid to the point of shaking in terror and then they will no longer be missing. The bad leadership had driven people from Israel, from the Lord, from the vision, and these new leaders would restore them. But how would they do it and even more important what was it that brought the people to this state in the beginning?

This texture forms almost an antiphonal approach in that one side of the bad leadership does this while the good side answer the same issue but in a new way. It is an exercise in contrasts. The evil shepherds are destroying and scattering the sheep in verse 1. The Lord's answer to this is that he will gather them back and a sign of this will be—they will not only come back but they will be fruitful and multiply in verse 3. Then the rebuke turns to how these bad leaders had failed in verse 2; they scattered the flock (notice this scattering is repeated twice) simply by not attending to them, not paying attention to them. The crux of the matter is that the leaders had failed by not paying attention to and taking care of the people. They were paying attention to something or someone else, in this text it does not matter who or what was taking their attention. The point is it was not on the people or the flock or the sheep of his pasture. The good leaders will be raised up; they will be developed and put over them both for the sake of authority and for the sake of paying attention to them and caring for them. This new way of leading will bring them back and it will relieve them of their terror and fear. People who are not under the cloud of fear can live freer, produce more, and even serve others. In this way, they will be fruitful and multiply, which was part of the original command from the garden. The issue here for leadership is that God has a way of leadership that is considered good and it is in serving the people by tending and caring for them, which should produce security and fruitfulness so they can multiply. Multiply in what way? This may be a question for another day. However, it would include multiplying who one is and what one does in life and leadership. There is more here in Jeremiah but for the moment this study moves on to another prophet.

Ezekiel 34 is a much longer pericope of rebuke to the shepherds but uses a slightly different form. In this extended metaphor is a summary of the themes and perspectives that dominate the prophetic understanding of leadership from the perspective of this pastoral language (Laniak, 2006). This pericope uses inner texture in its development of this rebuke. There is a repetitive texture with progressive texture used in contrasts and there is even a cause and effect argument in this section. The word "shepherd" is used here 11 times with "flock" used 9 times and "sheep" used 5 times. The focus here in these contrasts as well is on good and evil shepherds and their impact on the flock or the sheep who are the people in Israel. The cause and effect is found in verse 7 and 8 where the Lord says, "Therefore you shepherds … As I live', declares the Lord" and then He goes on to describe what He is going to do as a result of their bad shepherding. The first contrast is found in verse 2, where the shepherds have been feeding themselves instead of feeding the flock. However, in verse 10, it is found that the shepherds were actually consuming the flock itself. They had not only neglected the flock but they were actually working against the flock, they were the direct cause of the problem with the sheep being destroyed. The second contrast is found in verse 6 where the flock had been scattered and no one was there to search for them. There was no one to care for and look out for the sheep, for the people of Israel. These leaders were doing something else but here we are told what they are doing: they are feeding themselves, they are focused on themselves.

Then the ultimate contrast is found in verses 7 and 8 wherein the Lord says now this is what he is going to do in contrast to the previous shepherds who are being replaced by the Lord Himself. This section pivots on these two verses with contrast of lists before and after in a progression from bad to good leadership. Part of this progression can be seen in Table 4.2.

The prophet describes the shepherds and how they had failed with some instruction on what they should have done but now the Lord intervenes and contrasts how He will lead as a shepherd.

In verse 9, the Lord begins this description by taking the sheep and the job of shepherd or leader from the shepherds. He begins the contrast in verse 11 that He will search for the sheep and He will bring them back and He will feed them and in this process is found in verse 15 that the Lord will lead them and bring them to rest or peace. Then in verse 16 He will bring them back and heal them and strengthen them. However, at the end of the verse He brings judgment by destroying those who have become fat and strong. The shepherds are not only rejected but they will be judged for the destruction of the flock of God. Leadership is seen here as a very important task that has God's attention. These leaders failed in leadership by focusing on themselves and self-exaltation at the expense of their followers. The leaders were to care for, feed, gather, heal, and strengthen the people while leading them with gentleness not severity. These leaders utterly failed but the Lord stepped in and brought effective leadership by being the shepherd to the people by gathering, feeding, and healing them.

**Table 4.2** Contrasts of shepherding from bad leadership

| Ezekiel 34 | Shepherds | Contrast |
|---|---|---|
| 2 | Are feeding themselves | They should feed the flock |
| 3 | Eat the fat and clothe self without feeding the flock | |
| 4 | Did not strengthen the sick or heal the diseased | |
| 4 | Did not seek the lost | |
| 4 | Dominated them with force and severity | |
| 5–6 | Scattered and they became food for others | You did not seek for them |

## The Failure of Moses

In addition, Moses fails in his leadership at one point late in his life and as a result he was not allowed to go into the Promised Land. Moses was a great, larger-than-life leader. Yet he had a few flaws and these were enough to keep him from finishing well. The failure in Moses' leadership is found in Numbers 20:8–12 wherein Moses is told by the Lord to speak to the rock to produce water. In the past one other time, Moses was to strike the rock for water but this time he was to speak to it. Instead of speaking to the rock though Moses spoke to the people in anger, "Listen now you rebels; shall we bring forth water for you out of this rock" (Numbers 20:11)? He spoke against the people instead of to the rock and spoke harshly to them in a question. Contempt is heard in this question of Moses; in that one word, the act of name in calling them "rebels," Moses summed up years of frustration but it was actually he who rebelled at the moment; Moses lost the respect for those he led and God no longer felt Moses could lead them to their homeland (Brown, 2013). Moses had changed in his heart from the servant of the Lord and to the people to the commander of rebels. He had disobeyed the Lord not only in the act concerning the rock but also in the attitude change from servant leading servants to a rebel leader. Nevertheless, at the end of his life, Moses has one more positive aspect to his leadership that is found at the end of the Pentateuch in Deuteronomy 34:9, "Joshua the son of Nun was filled with the spirit of wisdom, for Moses had laid his hands on him; and the sons of Israel listened to him." Moses mentored Joshua for many years and in doing so he raised up an effective successor. Effective leadership needs to be passed on for a legacy of leadership. Part of Moses' success as a leader was having a successor who continued to lead successfully. So, even though Moses did not finish all the way to the end he continued to influence Israel through his leadership for another generation. In this end of Moses' leadership it is seen that attitude matters and issues of the heart are important to biblical leaders. It is also seen that part of success in leadership is having a successor who will continue to lead well.

## Servant Leadership or Shepherd Leadership

In this context comes the issue of leadership in the Old Testament—is it servant leadership or shepherd leadership or does it include issues from other models like charismatic leadership? Is there a difference between these two concepts of servant and shepherd in the Hebrew Scriptures? From these positive and negative pictures of the Old Testament emerge several important ideas for servant leadership including issues of humility, overcoming fear, confidence, and failure. Some are positive and some are negative but these are real-life dilemmas for leaders that if addressed before the disaster can bring good fruit. These attributes can be considered and developed to add strength to the model of servant leadership.

## Leadership Lessons from the Old Testament

Shepherds were the lowest and least desired of occupations. It was from this place of humility and lack of recognition that the leader was to serve. These leaders learned to overcome fear and difficult circumstances and even failure. In addition, these Old Testament leaders were careful to follow divine directives in fulfilling their calling as leaders. In the Old Testament, leaders were often called servants of the Lord but this usually implied service to a group of people as well. At other times in many places the leaders were called shepherds. However, it was found that in many of the places shepherd and servant leadership coincided with shepherd leadership having a high priority on serving and caring for people especially followers. In this context though there were found several areas for added nuance to servant leadership especially in the area of internal character development and how that is done. This development can even happen in the context of hardship and suffering as seen in several leaders and their development in the Old Testament. These concepts will be more fully developed in later sections of this study.

# Conclusion

Many highly diverse texts have been researched in this section with adding new insights for biblical leadership and for biblical servant leadership. Some of these insights come from peering into some of the failures of even great leaders with some who finished well and some who did not finish well. This study has examined the leadership of known leaders, like Joseph, and unknown leaders, like Barzillai, as well as leaders of renown, like Moses, and leaders who failed many times, like Samson. There were insights gleaned from stories like that of Esther as well as instructions or rather instructions in the context of rebuke as found in Jeremiah. These insights include issues like learning to overcome the human tendency toward greed and self-exaltation early in the process of leadership. Other issues include the reality that attitude counts and can help or hinder one in leading and serving others. There are large lists that can be drawn from this study of the Old Testament alone. There are even many more leaders and texts in this section of Scripture that can be studied like the Psalms or Proverbs as well as leaders like Deborah or Daniel. The over-arching idea found in these texts is that good leaders care for, tend to, and serve other people as servants of the Lord and shepherds of the people. Nevertheless, there is more work to be done in the life and teachings of Jesus as well as study in the rest of the New Testament teachings on leadership. Of note though is that this current study is only a portion of what is needed in this research for a biblical model of leadership.

# References

Akinyele, O. (2009). Queen Esther as a Servant Leader in Esther 5:1–8. *Journal of Biblical Perspectives in Leadership, 2*(2), 51–79.

Ayers, M. (2006). Towards a Theology of Leadership. *Journal of Biblical Perspectives in Leadership, 1,* 3–27.

Bauchman, V. (2013). *Joseph and the Gospel of Many Colors.* Wheaton, IL: Crossway.

Brown, E. (2013). *Leadership into the Wilderness: Authority and Anarchy in the Book of Numbers.* New Milford, CT: Maggid Books.

Childs, B. S. (1975). *The Book of Exodus*. Philadelphia, PA: The Westminster Press.

Clinton, J. R. (2012). *The Making of a Leader*. Colorado Springs, CO: NavPress.

Collins, J. C. (2001). *Good to Great: Why Some Companies Make the Leap—And Others Don't*. New York, NY: Harper Business.

Davidson, J. (2014). Women in the Old Testament Leadership Principles. In S. Bell (Ed.), *Servants and Friends: A Biblical Theology of Leadership* (pp. 259–275). Berrien Springs, MI: Andrews University Press.

Fee, G., & Stuart, D. (2014). *How to Read the Bible for All It's Worth: A Guide to Understanding the Bible*. Grand Rapids, MI: Zondervan.

Gane, B. (2014). Nehemiah: The Servant Leader. In S. Bell (Ed.), *Servants and Friends: A Biblical Theology of Leadership* (pp. 245–257). Berrien Springs, MI: Andrews University Press.

Guinness, O. (2003). *The Call: Finding and Fulfilling the Central Purpose of Your Life*. Nashville, TN: W Publishing.

Janzen, W. (2000). *Exodus* (Vol. 2). Scottdale, PA: Herald Press.

Laniak, T. S. (2006). *Shepherds After My Own Heart: Pastoral Traditions and Leadership in the Bible*. Downers Grove, IL: InterVarsity Press.

Lasor, W. S., Hubbard, D. A., & Bush, F. W. (1996). *Old Testament Survey: The Message, Form and Background of the Old Testament*. Grand Rapids, MI: Wm. B. Eerdmans Publishing Company.

Moskala, J. (2014). The Historical Books. In S. Bell (Ed.), *Servants and Friends: A Biblical Theology of Leadership* (pp. 65–85). Berrien Springs, MI: Andrews University Press.

Patterson, K. A. (2003). *Servant Leadership: A Theoretical Model*. Paper presented at the Servant Leadership Roundtable.

Peterson, P. B. (2014). The Prophets. In S. Bell (Ed.), *Servants and Friends: A Biblical Theology of Leadership* (pp. 103–122). Berrien Springs, MI: Andrews University Press.

Robbins, V. K. (1996). *Exploring the Texture of Texts: A Guide to Socio-Rhetorical Interpretation*. Harrisburg, PA: Trinity Press International.

Stevens, M. E. (2012). *Leadership Roles in the Old Testament: King, Prophet, Priest, Sage*. Eugene, OR: Cascade Books.

Wibberding, J. R. (2014). Wisdom Literature and the Psalms. In S. Bell (Ed.), *Servants and Friends: A Biblical Theology of Leadership* (pp. 87–101). Berrien Springs, MI: Andrews University Press.

Willimon, W. H. (2002). Back to the Burning Bush. *Christian Century, 119*(9), 7.

Witherington, B. (2007). *Letter and Homilies for Hellenized Christians: A Socio-Rhetorical Commentary on 1–2 Peter*. Downers Grove, IL: InterVarsity Press.

# 5

# Servant Leadership in the Life of Jesus

Jesus is the ultimate leader in that He is God come in the flesh. Therefore, we can learn from Him, and though He is omniscient, He has chosen to teach and model certain ways of living. In Jesus is found the example of a servant leader who, though fully divine, took on humanity and the human experience. He did this to redeem us from our sins and this is paramount in all of Christian theology. Nevertheless, He did at least two other things during His residence on this earth.

First, Jesus gives many instructions on multiple issues in the context of His day though these are taught in such a way that these instructions are timeless truths. He teaches about eternal issues and salvation, again, these are paramount in the New Testament. Then He teaches about issues that relate to our sojourn here on the earth among society. He teaches about economics, marriage and family issues, proper motivations, and leadership among many other topics. He is concerned in the gospels and in the first chapter of Acts about developing leaders in the training of the 12, and there are even 70 close disciples at times. He gives them and by extension everyone instructions about leadership that are theoretical and practical. Second, He lives an example of life, relationships, and leadership, and then we are told to imitate His example. He is the pattern or role model for leadership. In this pattern, servant leadership is seen and

© The Author(s) 2018
S. Crowther, *Biblical Servant Leadership*, Christian Faith Perspectives in
Leadership and Business, https://doi.org/10.1007/978-3-319-89569-7_5

discussed but is this the same as the twenty-first-century model? If it is servant leadership, does it expand the present model with its seven virtuous constructs and three goals or does it critique it? Then the final question is whether He gives more that goes beyond servant leadership in its present form.

# Instructions About Serving

Jesus gives instructions about serving to His disciples, and today as these are studied, it brings the advantage of listening to these conversations that are filled with wisdom and divine directives. Many of these directives are found to be countercultural to first century as well as twenty-first-century cultures and societies. In addition, at some points in these teachings they become counterintuitive as well. It seems like they are opposite to what one should do in a leadership role. However, in this way, these concepts would fit well with servant leadership. This study will examine four texts of the teaching of Jesus about leadership, but this is only a beginning. There are many more texts that could be chosen for this analysis and they should be chosen and examined in the future for a more nuanced understanding of the instructions from Jesus on leadership.

## Mark 10

In Mark 10, Jesus teaches the disciples to become servants to all. Is this a leadership issue or a life issue or is there some connection between the two? In this text, in Mark 10:35–45, Jesus had just told the disciples the third time about his coming death and how the Jewish leaders will mock Him as well as kill Him. Then the next conversation here is the question from James and John about how to be at Jesus' right- and left-hand sides in His Kingdom. It is important to point out here that the disciples were not aware of the implications of Jesus' coming death. They were looking for and expecting Jesus to be a military Messiah and to throw off the yoke of the Roman military machine and set up Israel as the center of all kingdoms on earth. This was quite a vision that was held by many Jews of the day generally but it was wrong. It was so wrong that Jesus corrected it at several points and these corrections were remembered by the disciples after the Day of Pentecost when they finally understood about His Messiahship.

In this story, the disciples were moving in the wrong direction with their questions. The disciples were perplexed at many points in their connection to Jesus and His teachings. In the previous encounter in this same chapter Jesus told them that it was difficult for this rich man to enter the Kingdom of God. In their thinking, if one was rich that person was close to God due to the blessing of wealth, which was seen as a sign of closeness to God, and the poor were considered to be distant from God. They were greatly perplexed when they found out that this rich man would not enter the kingdom of God. In their perplexity, Jesus told them about His death and their response was to ask for favored seats in His Kingdom. They did not understand His less-than-subtle message here about the way of the kingdom.

James and John ask for permission to sit at His right- and left-hand sides, and this begins a conversation that ends with Jesus explaining this concept about giving and serving. The key to life is not self-exaltation as was the thinking of society at this time. These are Jesus' most clear teachings on leadership, and in this teaching He redefined the vocabulary of leadership and He taught them how to lead in the Kingdom of God (Wilkes, 1998). This new way of leading was in response to the questions of James and John in their desire to sit in the exalted position. This is a very human tendency to have the place of privilege and power. The disciples are arguing among themselves about their own order of precedence, which leads to Jesus teaching on the paradoxical reversal of standards (Hooker, 1999). Martin Luther says that God hides Himself under opposites (Althaus, 1966). Jesus redirected their passion for position and gave them a new path, an unusual path to greatness in leading. Jesus responded to the disciples' mistaken notions about leadership and His teaching cuts through the superfluous issues of current leadership practices and moves quickly to the heart of the matter (Young, 2009). They wanted the positions of greatness but did not actually ask to be great; that might have been too bold. Some even suggest that the ensuing discussion about who would be the greatest was prompted by the thought of Jesus' death and who would replace Him, but then Jesus shares a teaching that will force them to rethink the values that characterize a true leader (Young, 2009). Jesus cuts to the core issue of the concepts of leadership and greatness.

The text of Mark 10:42–45 contains the core of the teaching of Jesus on leadership. The methods used here will be inner texture of Socio-Rhetorical Interpretation. The inner texture of the text resides in the features in the language of the text, like repetition of words or dialogue; it is the texture of the medium of communication (Robbins, 1996). De Silva (2004) says that inner texture is about the threads that the author has woven together to create meaning. In addition, grammatical analysis of historical grammatical method will be used to examine some of the words and sentences. Grammatical analysis is to understand the words we are reading (De Silva, 2004). Then finally, Inductive Bible Study will be used to examine issues like contrasts. An emphasis of Inductive Bible Study is the form of the text identifying literary structures showing how the structure forms the meaning of the text and one of these areas is that of contrast, that is, the association of opposites and the difference that the writer desires to emphasize (Bauer & Traina, 2014).

In this short pericope, there are several words that are repeated and these words become the focus of this text. Great is used twice and servant or its derivatives is used four times. The first section discusses greatness, but the second section discuses becoming a servant. Then it is apparent that Jesus uses particular words carefully here, like these Gentile rulers are considered rulers and these rulers exercise authority over others. Then He connects the words of great and first in this discussion. Notice that there are a series of contrasts here that form the core of the teaching on leadership. In addition, there are two examples held up here as role models. The first is a negative one, the Gentile rulers. The second is a positive one and this is Jesus. Notice again the use of contrast here. In the conclusion there is a chiasm. Chiasm's are found in literature and are named after the Greek letter for "X," *chi*. It is a sentence or sentences that use the same or similar topics twice and yet reverse the order. It is a pneumonic device for memory but it is also used to focus attention on its teaching. The chiasm here is found right at the end of the pericope. Notice the structure here of this teaching (Fig. 5.1):

There is also an opening, middle, and closing pattern from the inner texture here. Verse 42 is the opening which discusses the Gentile rulers then the middle is found in verse 43a with a statement of contrast—"But

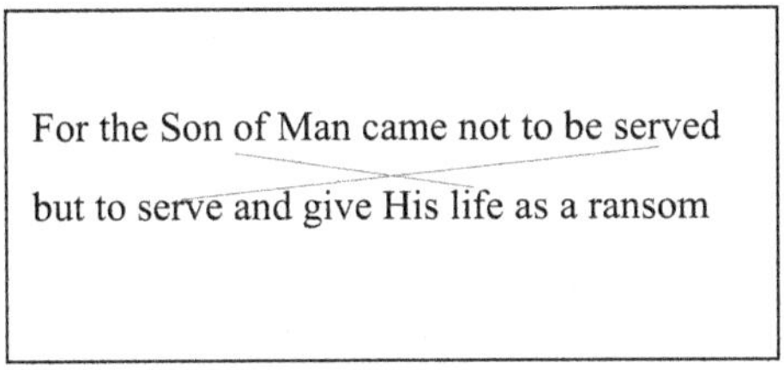

For the Son of Man came not to be served

but to serve and give His life as a ransom

**Fig. 5.1** Chiasm from Mark 10:45

**Table 5.1** Mark 10:42–45 patterns

| Scripture | Repetition | Open-M-Closing | Contrasts | Key words |
|---|---|---|---|---|
| 10:42 | Great | Opening | | Considered, over |
| 10:43a | | Middle | Not among you | |
| 10:43b | Great, servant | Closing | But whoever | Must be |
| 10:44 | Slave | Closing | | First |
| 10:45 | Served, serve | Closing | But to serve | Ransom |

it shall not be so among you." Then the final section is verses 43b–45 ending with the chiasm. These contrasts permeate this pericope from the overall level, like in verse 43a to the small level as in the chiasm in verse 45. The implication here is that Gentile leadership, which was the prominent model of leadership in this time period, was totally different, even opposite from the model of leadership that Jesus taught and lived. In that Jesus moves the discussion to Gentile rulers; this section is clearly about leadership. The later sections of servant are in contradistinction to these rulers. As a contrast they would both need to talk about the same issue. The issue is being a ruler or leadership. Table 5.1 shows these concepts together.

Jesus takes great care to contrast Gentile leadership with servant leadership. This is a clear declaration of servant leadership. First, it is of note that Jesus does not rebuke the disciples for wanting to be great. He actually encourages this desire for greatness. Nevertheless, in this kind of leading, greatness looks different and has a different path than the norm. These Gentile rulers are considered rulers. This word "considered" means to think or seem to be something (Friberg & Friberg, 1994). They seem to be leaders but are they to be imitated as leaders? The implication is that they are not the models to follow for a pattern of leadership. Then notice that they exercise authority over, they are not with the followers in collaboration, they are over them, and they use their authority as one over another.

The repetitions change just after the middle as it moves into the closing. The focus moves from greatness to serving. Wanting to be great is good but the focus now needs to change to becoming a servant in how to become a great leader. At the same time these repetitions change; the contrasts begin to appear. The first contrast is in verse 43a and it is the large contrast in the full teaching in this pericope. This is the contrast between Gentile rulers and servant leaders. These are two opposite ends of the spectrum in leadership. One focuses on the greatness of the person and this person's authority, while the other one focuses on the person becoming a servant and then serving others. This contrast moves quickly into another contrast in verse 43b. This is the transition from greatness to servanthood. Greatness is a good goal but there is a new and opposite path. Notice here that his greatness is not an appearance of greatness but it is becoming great and the process is now in becoming a servant. It does not begin with serving but first it begins with becoming a servant. It is an ontological change first. This shift then is a shift in thinking, priorities, and even a shift in being or *ontos*. In verse 44, Jesus restates this concept but replaces some of the words. He replaces greatness with first and servant with slave. This word "first" instead of "greatness" means first of several (Friberg & Friberg, 1994). This word is transitioning the focus from self to others and it is a position among many instead of a place that is over others. The word "servant" is one who renders help to another, whereas slave is one who is in obedience to another (Friberg & Friberg, 1994). These do not cancel each other but instead work together in this person who helps others and this is in obedience to God. This is the divine intention for leaders. Then notice that to be great one must become servant of all. This is not a suggestion; this is what must happen for this path to greatness to work. In addition, the word here is not that one should serve but that the leader must become servant. It is an ontological change; it is an internal issue first, then comes the giving and the serving.

The final contrast is found in the final verse and it is also the chiasm. Here Jesus says that even the Son of man came in this way. He is stating that this is the reason or explanation for what He is saying (Friberg & Friberg, 1994). He came and led in this way and this is the pattern to follow and this is the foundation for this teaching about servant leadership. This is the contrast between being served as king or ruler and serving others. However, this contrast goes even farther in that it went beyond serving to giving, a giving of Himself to rescue (ransom) others.

The full impact of this teaching from Jesus can only been seen in the repetitions and the intensity of these contrasts along with the implications as He changes the words throughout this teaching. Jesus is the model for leadership here. It is opposite of the normal Gentile path to greatness. It is a path to greatness but a path that includes others and is not over as much as it is among others. Then the path is to become a servant in obedience to God. This is the divine perspective on leadership. Once one becomes a servant that leader is then to serve others and even to give of self to others. The focus changes to giving of self rather than preserving or exalting self. The leader today cannot give self as a ransom for others redemptively like Jesus did. However, this word is not necessarily "redemptive" here in this text. Hooker (1999) says that this is not the same word used in the Old Testament as an offering for sin. This concept of ransom is a transaction where one brings another out of bondage (Crowther, 2009). The leader then serves others in helping them in some very profound ways bringing help and freedom to them.

In this text, there are many issues of servant leadership that confirm and possibly expand the theory. This teaching develops servant leadership as countercultural and a path toward greatness in leadership among others who are with them. It gives a path of leadership that involves a focus on others, helping them in some profound ways bring freedom to them. It pushes beyond serving though to give of self and it focuses on becoming a servant as well as doing service. This is seen in the contemporary model of the virtue theory of servant leadership. However, here it is emphasized. In addition, it moves past helping others to doing it in obedience to the Lord and as a result of the call on the life of the leader.

## Matthew 28

In Matthew 28, Jesus teaches the disciples how to impart this way of kingdom living to others. Right at the very end of the gospel of Matthew after His resurrection, Jesus makes one final statement to His disciples. In Matthew 28:18–20, Jesus gives a command about how to advance this kingdom message to His disciples just before He leaves and returns to heaven. This final message is significant in that it gives a detailed explanation of how to finish the task that Jesus began while he was here on the earth. Matthew offers a direct charge to the disciples of Jesus who will become the movement's leaders, it involves authority to carry out the mission and it involves disciples making disciples, which along with teaching is the fundamental function of gospel leadership (Agosto, 2005).

In this text is found a progressive texture of inner texture where the message gives a command with multiple components. Then there is argumentative texture of inner texture as well wherein the disciples are told what to do in response to the position of Jesus in authority. There are some important words here as well including "commanded" and "end of the age." These are final words to the new leaders of the movement on how to continue and lead in this Messianic movement.

Jesus begins with a cause and effect argument. He has all authority and it has been given to Him. This is an important point in that the inference is that this authority was given to Him by the Father and further that all authority is God's authority. If this line of thinking is followed, it means that all authority is derived authority with the exception of God's authority. God is the source of authority and all authority is derived from Him. Possibly, this is the very thing that the devil tried to steal through the temptation of Jesus in the wilderness, the authority of God. Authority is a major issue in leadership. All authority is from God and it is delegated to others; therefore, authority needs to be used properly as an external gift rather than as a possession. Since this full authority had been given to Jesus, as a result of this or the end of the argument is therefore go. All leadership authority is derived authority. Now Jesus is telling them to use this authority in a certain way, to lead others in becoming disciples. Authority like talents can be misused, but here is instruction on at least one way to properly use authority.

As the instruction continues, Jesus gives them a practical message that is progressive; it has parts that build on each other. First, the disciples are to go to others and then make disciples of them, help them become a follower of Christ. Second, they are to baptize these new followers indicating that they are beginning a new way of life. Finally, these new disciples are to be taught everything Jesus had told them to observe or follow and to teach them about the things that were commanded. Then finally Jesus said He would be with them until the end of the age. How does one make disciples? By going to them, then baptizing them, bringing them into a new way of life, and teaching them. Then Jesus promised His presence with them until the end of the age, the age that we are yet in. This mandate is continuous and continues today.

There are several leadership issues here. First, it can be seen that this leadership is focused on others and helping them in an ongoing way. Specific instructions are given as to how to lead another as a disciple and it involves going to them or initiating the service to them. It has ongoing components of focus on the follower in baptizing and teaching them. Then there is the issue of authority. God has all authority and the Father gives it to the Son. The Son then sends the disciples as a result of that authority. Here is seen the proper use of and submission to authority in the doing of leading.

The connection to servant leadership is seen here in this focus on others. It includes not only a focus on others but also a seeking them out to serve them and an ongoing process of longitudinal service. This confirms servant leadership but it could also expand it in seeking out those to serve and serving them in profound long-term ways. However, there is the issue of authority which appears to be outside of the contemporary model. Is the proper use and response to authority an issue that needs to be included in a model of leadership? The pattern is seen here and Jesus makes a point of pivoting on this issue of authority as the argument for the disciples going and serving in this way. Inherent in this message is the focus on followers but it is also in pursuit of the mission in making disciples of all the *ethnos* or people groups on the earth. Where does this focus on mission fit into leadership or into servant leadership? Can servant leaders focus on mission by focusing on followers? This would fit into the third goal of focusing on the organization but does the mission need more central attention? This is a question that needs development in the search for biblical servant leadership.

## John 13, John 21

Then in the gospel of John, Jesus models servanthood in washing the feet of the disciples and He teaches them how to become servants to others. In the gospel of John, we find several stories that are distinct from those of the Synoptic Gospels. These two stories are in this group of stories unique to John. In the first story, Jesus is found with His disciples in the upper room where He takes a moment in the midst of all the different events to wash the feet of the disciples. Here Jesus chooses a servant's towel to express His leadership and His love to His disciples. In the second story, Jesus is questioning and instructing Peter on how to lead others in this new movement.

In John 13:1–17, Jesus washes the feet of the disciples and gives them instructions about what He is doing and how they should follow His example. In this story is seen Jesus' towel of servanthood as the physical symbol of servant leadership, He met the physical and spiritual needs of the followers showing what servant leaders do (Wilkes, 1998). In this pericope, there is an open-middle-closing of inner texture. The opening is in verse 1 when Jesus was considering the moment He was in and that this would be the last supper with His disciples. The middle is the event during the supper of Jesus washing their feet that goes from verse 2 to verse 11. Then in verse 11, Jesus explained about the foot-washing lesson and how they should respond, and this is the closing that continues to the end of this pericope.

In the repetitions of inner texture, there are several words that are used twice—"world," "loved," "Father," "God," "towel," and "greater." One word is used three times—"understand." Then one concept is used eight times in these verses and that is the concept of washing feet. This is the focal point of the message and Jesus wants them to understand what He is doing and He explains it using the concept of servant. There is also a narrational texture in the middle of this pericope where Peter and Jesus enter a conversation about washing feet. There is thematic contrast here as well. The contrast is between Judas, who is the one betraying Jesus for money and gain, and Jesus, who is becoming the servant to all including Judas the betrayer. Judas is trying to promote himself, while Jesus is pressing down to become the servant even to the one who is the betrayer.

The word "loved" is of particular interest here. Jesus expressed this love for them by serving them and providing an example of leading by serving. It says He loved them to the end in verse 1. To the end of what? This seems to be a dangling thought. To the end of His human life? This seems unlikely. In the Greek language, this is the end of some act or state but not a period of time, here in John 13:1 it is to the uttermost or completely (Bushnell, 2001). He loved them to the end of how they can be loved. The NIV translates it this way. He showed them the full extent of His love. The motive here is love the core issue of servant leadership in the virtuous model of the twenty-first century.

The message of Jesus is clearly about showing the disciples the way to lead by serving. He mentioned that He indeed was their Master and teacher yet He washed their feet as an example for them. It was important to Jesus that the disciples saw and understood this truth; He even took special time to explain it to Peter with more details. It was also important that the later readers of Scripture saw that this was done in the context of the betrayal of Judas. Serving is not contingent on worthiness.

Servant leadership is seen here in this text as Jesus is motivated by great love to serve those He is leading, even those that are less than worthy of this love or leadership. This serving is washing their feet that is truly a job for servants. The disciples did not understand however; Jesus took extra measures for them to understand. He was the Master and Lord and their teacher; yet, He was their servant and this is an example that they are to follow in their leadership of others. This is not a theology of foot washing, but it is using this physical, clear example to help them develop a theology of leadership of servant leadership; now blessed are you if you do this and lead as a servant. This is a clear example of Jesus teaching and modeling servant leadership that reinforces the concepts as found in the contemporary model of servant leadership.

In John 21, the disciples have gone fishing after the resurrection of Christ. In this short pericope from verse 15 to verse 18, Jesus is having a very direct discussion with Peter. Peter and Jesus and some of the other disciples had just finished breakfast yet Jesus wanted to talk to Peter about love and leadership. There are several questions and words that are repeated in this section as part of inner texture. Then some of the words are changed slightly though they have similar meanings.

Jesus asks the same question three times with slight variations about Peter's love for him. The first time He asks Peter do you love me more than these. There is great speculation about the meaning of this reference to these. Possibly the fish or fishing but He is comparing Peter's love for Jesus with something else. Peter responds that he does love Jesus more than these. Then Jesus gives him instructions about His sheep (people) once Peter declares his love. The instruction that Peter is receiving depends on his love, it is a love issue and a motive issue. He then tells Peter to feed His lambs or little ones, young ones. In the process of this interaction, Jesus changes the instructions slightly each time. Jesus charges Peter to feed (*boske*) the sheep and the lambs and to shepherd (*pomaine*) the sheep (Maloney, 1998).

The second question is simply the question of Peter's love for Jesus and Peter again answers in the affirmative. This time Peter is told to shepherd the sheep. Then the same question is asked a third time with some variation in the Greek wording but the same question. This time Peter is disturbed and he expresses this dismay but Jesus simply tells him this time to feed His sheep.

There are several important issues here. First is seen that love is connected to leadership. Then it becomes apparent that Jesus is giving specific instructions about this leadership for the young and for the mature people of God. The leader is to feed the people. There are many examples of how shepherds feed the sheep or lambs. They do not feed them like you would feed a child, but they help them find places that are good and protect them while they are there. This concept of shepherd would be in the area of intertexture of Socio-Rhetorical Interpretation. Intertexture is the text's representation of and use of phenomena in the world outside of the text and the interaction with issues like historical issues, other texts, roles, or institutions (Robbins, 1996). Here, the text interacts with something known by all in this time period and that is a shepherd. Especially Jews were familiar with this comparison since the Old Testament already used this picture of a shepherd of sheep as a leader on many different levels including prophets, kings, and elders. The best of the human kings was David, but he was associated with a different term for leader—that of "shepherd"—and this was a term used by God for the sort of leader that David was to become and it was also used for leaders in the tribes of Israel (Burns, Shoup, & Simmons, 2014). Then the leader is also to shepherd or to tend to the sheep. This has the sense of caring for them.

The leader is to lead motivated by love according to Jesus. However, here in this text, it is love for Jesus not for the sheep or people. Is this transferred to the sheep in some way or is this a place for the expansion of servant leadership? It must be noted though that these shepherds had a very special attachment to the sheep (Burns et al., 2014). Possibly, this is an unspoken understanding between Peter and Jesus and the original readers. Nevertheless, it still remains that the focus of this text is love for Jesus. Peter as a leader is to feed, to bring help and protection to the people of God and he is to care for them. The leader is to be shepherd in the pattern of the Old Testament shepherds who were sent by God to lead on different levels but to lead by guiding and caring. This fits well with contemporary servant leadership. However, the one area that may need further research is this concept of a leader feeding the followers. This is an analogy or a picture and it implies leading from behind through relationship not as a director or driver. Shepherds like these and like Jesus were willing to give their lives for the sheep; by precept and example, Jesus taught servant leadership (Johnston, 2014). The shepherds were servants in connection to the sheep. Nevertheless, this concept of shepherd includes the concept of guiding and protecting. Are these part of a biblical servant leadership and if so do they fit the existing model? Protecting may well fit the model but further research is needed for the guiding aspect as found in the shepherd analogy.

## Luke 7

In Luke, Jesus uses the leadership of a military leader of Rome to provide an example of how to lead. In Luke 7:1–10, Jesus is in Capernaum speaking to the crowds when someone comes to appeal for His help, which begins this story. In this text is found a narrational texture of the voices of Jesus and the centurion. Narrational texture resides in the voices in which the words of the text speak through a narrator or attributed speech (Robbins, 1996). There is also repetition in the inner texture of the words of centurion and servant. This is a story about the centurion and his servant with interaction from Jesus. The core of the message is in Jesus' amazement in the way that the centurion responds to Jesus about his servant. This statement that Jesus was amazed could be properly translated as to wonder or even to admire (Friberg & Friberg, 1994).

Jesus is on His way to the centurion's house to heal his servant. The centurion is a Gentile, yet Jesus responds to this invitation. On the way a messenger comes from the centurion with a message for Jesus. This is the core issue captured in this narrational texture of this text. The message is straightforward in that Jesus does not need to come all the way to the house, He can just say the word and the servant will be healed. This is amazing enough that a Gentile understood the issues of divine power through Jesus. It does not stop here though; the message continues as the centurion is speaking to Jesus through the messenger. The centurion even declares that he knows why this will work. He declares to Jesus that he is a man under authority and therefore he has authority. He knows that since Jesus is under authority to the Father He has authority even over diseases and this authority is not hindered by spatial distance. What an incredible revelation from this Gentile centurion! Even the spiritual Israelites did not understand this concept. Jesus stops. He was amazed and wondered at this centurion that could make this statement; maybe he even admired him. Then He speaks directly to the crowd saying that He had not seen such great faith even in Israel. What was this? Was this only an issue of faith in a spiritual sense? Jesus was endorsing this man's faith and his statements about authority. This man was a leader in the military. Somehow he understood authority and he was able to translate this knowledge and apply it to the healing of his servant. He was under authority; therefore, he had authority, and this authority gave him power. Clearly, Jesus was amazed at his faith for healing. However, he endorsed this man and this man had a simple message but it is also a leadership message. A leader must be under authority and then this leader will be able to use authority but it is also an issue of faith.

Does biblical leadership include an understanding of authority in being under authority and using authority properly? This is an important question in that the Scriptures have much to say about authority both divine and human. The theological roots of any biblical understanding of leadership must grow in the soil of God's authority; this authority though can be delegated to humans (Burns et al., 2014). Authority is an important issue and it is seen in coming to the surface here in this text but it rises to the surface in other texts as well. However, this brings a question to the forefront. Is the Bible too complex and too focused on other issues that it makes it difficult to develop a model of biblical leadership and only disparate concepts for leadership can be developed? There are some who would agree that only concepts could be found. Like Burns et al. (2014) who say that it is difficult or impossible to identify a single biblical model of leadership, at least in the way we conceive of a model, since there are so many biblical examples. This is difficult but it must be kept in mind that the jury is still out. We have yet to examine all of the examples and directives and endorsements of leadership in Scripture. In addition, this must be done carefully not accepting every biblical leader as an example. Even Moses had some bad qualities that need not be repeated and endorsed. Then there are Scriptures that give specific instructions and give clear examples of leaders to follow like Jesus who is the chief shepherd. This is complex and difficult and highly nuanced but it is worth the pursuit and the process.

## Jesus as the Example of Servant Leadership

### 1 Peter 2

This example of Jesus as a servant leader is explained by both Peter and Paul. Peter connects Jesus' leadership to that of the suffering servant in Isaiah 52. In 1 Peter 2:21–25, the author is speaking about suffering for Christ. He changes the focus from the follower to Christ Himself saying that He left us an example that we would follow in His steps. The material here is drawn from Isaiah's portrait of the suffering servant to show Christ as this suffering servant as an example for the believer to follow (Elliot, 2000).

The prominent word here is "suffering" but the recurring theme is Christ seen in the words of "Christ" but then also referring back to Him with the pronouns "he" or "him." This occurs nine times in this short passage. Then the image of sheep and shepherd reappears here as well. He is the example in suffering but could He be the example in leadership as well? We know from other texts that this is true. However, is it implied here? The word in this text refers to the exact pattern of alphabetic letters which children traced so they could learn their letters (Witherington, 2007). The context is discussing the believer following Jesus and following closely, and suddenly it changes to straying sheep and Jesus being the Shepherd and Overseer of our souls. Christ is held as the example here in suffering, and in leadership, the believer is to follow very close, and this example includes leading as a shepherd, caring for followers, and as an overseer who guides the followers (Crowther, 2013). In this text is seen Jesus setting the example for others to follow in suffering for others and as a shepherd leader who cares for the sheep. This confirms the issue of servant leadership but it brings the question to front again about this image of shepherd as leader. Is a shepherd leader a servant leader or is there more to this image? Then there is the question of guiding again in the image of overseer. This is the same word that is translated as "bishop" in other contexts. This text confirms and possibly expands the model of servant leadership.

## Phil 2

Paul explains the leadership of Jesus as a digression to servanthood and a progression to glory. Paul then exhorts the believers to follow this example in living and in leading. This section in Philippians 2:5–11 is written as a hymn. Within the social and cultural context of first-century Philippi the consensus is that this hymn was written as a religious response to the tyranny of Roman leadership, this text in Philippians develops an alternative exemplary model for leadership (Bekker, 2006). The text begins with an exhortation to the believer to have this same attitude as Christ. Notice here that this is not just talking about behavior; it is going deeper to areas of motive. Jesus Christ is being held up as the example of a different form of leadership that ultimately results in glory to God instead of glory to the leader. This Philippian hymn challenged the principles of shame and honor of Roman society offering an alternative set of values in contrast to those of the dominant culture offering an alternative vision of service-oriented leadership rooted in humility and common mutuality (Bekker, 2006).

In the text of 2:5–11 of Philippians is found several issues of the textures of Scripture. An important texture to observe here is the progressive texture of the digression and progression of Christ. In the midst of this texture there is a chiasm as well. Then there are some key words that need attention and some clear contrasts. There is more but this will suffice for this study for the moment. There are also several repetitions of inner texture. The prominent words are "God" four times and "Christ" or references to Him seven times and the word "form" three times. This text focuses on Jesus and His submission to God in humility and then God exalts Him. He humbled Himself by taking on a human form.

The progressive texture is found in this intentional self-humbling of Christ in the steps He took to the cross and then the progression of God exalting Him. It has the form of a downward direction in humility to the obedience of the cross then it turns upward as God exalts Him. First in verse 6, He was in the form of God but did not count this as something to be grasped. This word "form" means the appearance and the nature of something (Friberg & Friberg, 1994). Christ did not grasp this equality. Second, Christ emptied Himself. This word "kenosis" is the concept of self-emptying of one's will and becoming entirely receptive to God's will and Jesus Christ is the example of this process (Danley, 2009). He does not cease from divinity but He does not grasp it and in this He sets the example for others. Third, he takes the form of a servant. This is the appearance and the nature of a servant. Fourth, He takes on human form. He takes on human likeness and experiences life from the human place in the universe. He is not just a servant but He is divine and puts on the nature not only of a servant but of a human servant. Fifth, He humbled Himself. This is an action that he took—it was self-humbling, it was not an external need, it was an internal decision. Remember the exhortation here is not to understand the theology of Christ, but it is to adopt this same attitude and way of living and even leading as Christ did here. This call to humility includes the voluntary rejection of symbols and systems of power including prestige and privilege (Bekker, 2006). Sixth is His obedience even to the point of death on the cross. This is obedience to God and His purpose for His life in fulfilling the goal of submission to God. This is radical obedience in spite of the results.

This progressive texture takes a sudden turn with the word "therefore" in verse 9. What is getting ready to happen is a turn upward and it is no longer driven by Jesus but now this is done to Jesus by God. These actions to come are based upon the previous actions of Christ. First, God highly exalted Him. Those that humble themselves will be exalted by God in due time (1 Peter 5:6). Second, God exalted His name above every name and every tongue will confess. Jesus was vindicated as the one who is True and Right though He was rejected and crucified. In the book of Revelation, believers who overcome are given a new name (Revelation 2:17). This is a special gift to those who have overcome in heaven. Third, and finally, this ultimately is for the glory of God. Remember this attitude is to be in the leaders of Philippi and in believers today. There are six steps in the downward progression and three in the upward progression as seen in Table 5.2.

This way of thinking is to become the way or the attitude of the believer and the leader in contradistinction to the leadership way of the current culture. In this way, it is a countercultural model for leadership. Social and cultural texture of Socio-Rhetorical Interpretation in the area of final categories deals with seeing the context of the text and whether it is from a dominant or subculture or countercultural or other cultural viewpoint (Robbins, 1996). In the social and cultural texture of this text, it is seen to be countercultural forming an alternate way of life from the dominant culture.

In the text, leadership is seen in a servant model with many components of the servant leadership model. These include not grasping at identity and power but becoming a servant not just serving and humility. However, in some ways this moves beyond or even deepens the concepts of servant leadership. These concepts of self-emptying and obedience may seem radical and even that of identifying with other humans moving past sympathy to empathy may seem like too much. Nevertheless, this is

**Table 5.2** The progression of the life of Christ

| Downward progression | Therefore | Upward progression |
|---|---|---|
| Did not grasp | Change from self to God | Highly exalted him |
| Self-emptying | | Name and vindication |
| Servant form | | Glory to God |
| Human form | | |
| Humility | | |
| Obedience | | |

the exhortation of Paul in following the servant leadership example of Christ. Can servant leadership be expanded to include these components? These are internal issues and can be part of a virtues theory. How can that be done though in this contemporary context? Then there is the upside of the progression that God does in exalting, vindicating, and receiving glory. There is no doubt that Scripture clearly teaches that those who humble themselves will be exalted by God. Will God vindicate us and give us a new name, a new reputation? This is also possible but remember it is God who does this not the leader. Finally, it is seen that this is to the glory of God. What does leadership have to do with the glory of God? The goal of leadership is to accomplish the mission but the ultimate goal is to bring glory to God. In this text, the end result or the *telos* of this process is glory to God.

## Conclusion

Many different texts have been explored with various results and concepts to consider for leadership. Many of them confirm the contemporary virtuous model of servant leadership. However, there are a few areas that expand or even critique this model. It is found that Jesus' teachings and example exude servant leadership concepts. However, there were a few areas found that move beyond servant leadership. Some of these areas include the issue of the proper use of authority and the concept of shepherd leadership. Are these concepts already in this model in some way or are they needed to expand the model for it to be biblical servant leadership? There is more though in that there are concepts of giving of or emptying self. In addition, there is the issue of a mission focus and whether that is inherent in the model or if this concept critiques or expands the model. Finally, there is a deep expression of servant leadership in Philippians 2. Does this depth match or expand the modern theory of servant leadership? Then there is the issue of the teleology of leadership concerning the glory of God. Does this purpose of bringing glory to God need to be addressed in the model of leadership? There are many questions to be addressed. Many of these will be addressed in later chapters as we continue to search for answers concerning biblical leadership.

# References

Agosto, E. (2005). *Servant Leadership: Jesus & Paul.* St. Louis, MO: Chalice Press.

Althaus, P. (1966). *The Theology of Martin Luther.* Minneapolis, MN: Fortress Press.

Bauer, D. R., & Traina, R. A. (2014). *Inductive Bible Study: A Comprehensive Guide to the Practice of Hermeneutics.* Grand Rapids, MI: Baker Academic.

Bekker, C. J. (2006). *The Philippians Hymn (2:5–11) as an Early Mimetic Christological Model of Christian Leadership in Roman Philippi.* Paper presented at the Servant Leadership Research Roundtable.

Burns, J., Shoup, J., & Simmons, D. (Eds.). (2014). *Organizational Leadership: Foundations and Practices for Christians.* Downers Grove, IL: InterVarsity Press.

Bushnell, M. S. (2001). Thayer's *Greek-English Lexicon of the New Testament.* Complete and Unabridged. Being C. G. Grimm (1861–1868; 1879) and C. L. W. Wilke (1851) Clavis Novi Testamenti Translated, Revised, and Enlarged, by Joseph Henry Thayer, D.D., Hon. Litt.D., Professor of New Testament, Divinity School of Harvard University, 1889. Electronic Edition Generated and Owned by International Bible Translators (IBT), Inc., 1998–2000. Greek Formatting Modifications (Such as Adding Diacritical Accents) and Improvements Made by Michael S. Bushell, 2001.

Crowther, S. S. (2009). The Spirit of Service: Reexamining Servant Leadership in the Gospel of Mark. *Inner Resources for Leaders, 1*(3), 1–7.

Crowther, S. S. (2013). *Peter on Leadership: A Contemporary Exegetical Analysis.* Fayetteville, NC: Ontos Zoe Publishing.

Danley, D. A. (2009). Toward an Understanding of the Kenosis of Christ: A Proposed a Priori Constituent to Transformative Leadership Traits in Philippians 2:5–11 (Doctoral dissertation). *Dissertation Abstracts International: Section A, 71*(11). (UMI No. 3425736).

De Silva, D. (2004). *An Introduction to the New Testament: Contexts, Methods & Ministry Formation.* Downers Grove, IL: IVP Academic.

Elliot, J. H. (2000). *The Anchor Bible: I Peter.* New Haven, CT: Yale University Press.

Friberg, T., & Friberg, B. (1994). *Analytical Greek New Testament (GNM)* (2nd ed.). n.p.: Timothy and Barbara Friberg.

Hooker, M. (1999). *The Gospel According to Saint Mark: Black's New Testament Commentary.* London: A & C Black Publishers Ltd.

Johnston, R. M. (2014). The Gospels. In S. Bell (Ed.), *Servants and Friends: A Biblical Theology of Leadership* (pp. 147–162). Berrien Springs, MI: Andrews University Press.

Maloney, F. J. (1998). The Gospel of John. In D. J. Harrington (Ed.), *Sacra Pagina* (Vol. 4). Collegeville, MN: The Liturgical Press.

Robbins, V. K. (1996). *Exploring the Texture of Texts: A Guide to Socio-Rhetorical Interpretation.* Harrisburg, PA: Trinity Press International.

Wilkes, C. G. (1998). *Jesus on Leadership: Discovering the Secrets of Servant Leadership from the Life of Christ.* Lifeway Press: London.

Witherington, B. (2007). *Letter and Homilies for Hellenized Christians: A Socio-Rhetorical Commentary on 1–2 Peter.* Downers Grove, IL: InterVarsity Press.

Young, H. L. (2009). *A Primer for Servant Leadership: Leading in the Right Direction.* BookSurge.

# 6

# Leadership in the New Testament

After the ministry of Jesus, the church continues this ministry of servant leadership in many different settings. These settings involve different people in different leadership situations and there are many examples as well as directives. The question is whether all of the examples are examples of servant leadership. Then there are also specific instructions for leaders from other leaders like Paul, Peter, James, and John. In the quest for biblical servant leadership, these different avenues will be explored looking for insights for leadership as well as confirmation, expansion, or critique of servant leadership. Do these different teachings and examples align with each other or are they diverse models and instructions? Could there be some diversity here? Is there another model of leadership that is biblical other than servant leadership and if so what is it? Burns, Shoup, and Simmons (2014) find transformational leadership in the texts of Scripture. Is there more than one model here or is there a new way to do an expanded model? In looking at these texts these issues will be explored.

© The Author(s) 2018
S. Crowther, *Biblical Servant Leadership*, Christian Faith Perspectives in
Leadership and Business, https://doi.org/10.1007/978-3-319-89569-7_6

# Servant Leadership in the Book of Acts

## Barnabas

Barnabas is the leader with the recognition and title needed for leadership in the church; but when he sees Paul rise as the leader, he allows Paul to take the lead. Barnabas is introduced in Acts 4:36–37 where he gives of his resources to the church in the time of need to provide for other people. Barnabas is a movement leader with possessions willing to give them up for the cause (Agosto, 2005). It can be seen from this same text that his name means son of encouragement or consolation. He had such an impact on people that they renamed him to declare his attributes. He was a comforter and a giver. This act is mentioned as a summary of the quality of life in the Christian community and this makes Barnabas in the eyes of the reader, an example of charity (Sauvagnat, 2014). In Acts 9:27, Barnabas becomes the advocate for Saul who had persecuted the church but now converted. He was the first in Jerusalem to embrace Saul who would become Paul. In Acts 11:22–26, Barnabas is sent by the Jerusalem leaders to Antioch since there was a new growing church movement there that included Gentiles. Their explanation for sending him was that he was a good man and full of the Holy Spirit. This word "good" speaks of good moral character (Friberg & Friberg, 1994). He was a man of character and a spiritual man. Then once he arrives in Antioch, he goes to find Saul who had returned to his hometown of Tarsus. Then for a whole year Saul and Barnabas led these new believers in Antioch. Luke presents Barnabas as a transformed man, a man of godly character (Sauvagnat, 2014). Barnabas went to find help and had the humility to know that this ministry was bigger than he could do or handle.

In Acts 13 and 14, Barnabas is seen with Paul and sent with Paul to the work of taking the gospel to other places. Barnabas appears to be the lead partner of the team until Cyprus. Here Saul's name is changed to Paul and from here on Paul is mentioned first and is the primary speaker of the group yet Barnabas continues with the group but as secondary to Paul. In Acts 15, Barnabas is in the Jerusalem council, and he and Paul together defend the gospel going to the Gentiles by recounting the miracles that God had done through them among the Gentiles. Finally there was a division between Paul and Barnabas over whether to take a team member who had already failed once. Paul did not want to take John Mark again but Barnabas did, so they parted ways and Barnabas went with Mark and Paul took Silas. Barnabas recruited and trained Paul, the great apostle, and Mark, the writer of the gospel with his name, and Barnabas demonstrates the principle of empowering others (Sauvagnat, 2014).

Barnabas is a morally good man with godly character, and this is what qualified him for his early leadership assignments. He has the humility to help and develop and encourage others even when they surpass him in leadership. He was willing to take a chance on those others had rejected. His was a leader of empowering others even when he did not receive the glory for it. Barnabas would be a good role model for a servant leader.

## Aeneas

Aeneas also intersects with Paul's life, and though he is afraid of Paul, he still serves him and brings him revelation of the new things of the Kingdom of God. Aeneas is seen in only one text in Acts 9 in verses 10–19. He is an important person for Paul, which makes him an important person to those of us who read the New Testament. First, Aeneas receives a vision from the Lord where he is instructed to go and minister to the great persecutor of the church. He resisted but the Lord insisted and he decided to go and minister to Paul. Once there with Paul, he prays for Paul's eyes and they get healed then Paul gets baptized. This is it. We do not see Aeneas again but he is a pivotal figure for the life of Paul. He is seen here serving one person at great risk to himself. He was concerned that Saul may still be persecuting the church, which would have meant imprisonment or possible death to Aeneas. Nevertheless, he went. Servant leaders can serve the one or the many; the point is serving and Aeneas is here doing this serving at great risk to himself. He was a servant leader in that he led Saul into the things of the Lord and brought him baptism and healing. Some servant leaders will become well known like Barnabas, while others may never be known as to who they are or what they have done, like Aeneas. This story of Aeneas would not have been known had not Luke and the Holy Spirit decided to put this event in the Book of Acts.

It adds value to the story in connecting the before and after Saul. It also has value for the reader to see behind the scenes and see some of the unsung servant leaders.

## Priscilla and Aquila

This couple shows up on the scene in the Book of Acts as tentmakers in the same profession as Paul. They quickly become valuable leaders in the movement as they serve some of the teachers of the movement, such as Apollos. Paul meets Aquila and Priscilla, a husband and wife who are believers in Corinth in Acts 18. They were from Rome but left under the command of Caesar for all Jews to leave. When Paul left Corinth for Asia, they went with him; only now they were known as Priscilla and Aquila. There appears to be a role reversal here in the lead of this marriage team. They came to Ephesus but Paul left for Antioch and left Priscilla and Aquila in Ephesus. Apollos came to Ephesus preaching eloquently about Jesus. However, he only knew part of the story. Priscilla and Aquila took him aside and explained to him the rest of the story. Apollos goes on to become a valuable leader for the church. Priscilla and Aquila serve others beginning with Paul with whom they share tent-making as a profession. They even travel with him. Once Apollos comes on the scene, they instruct him in a more perfect way in the understanding of the gospel and afterwards he becomes a great leader and speaker. This couple serves in the background as an example of servant leaders to help other leaders, to serve these other leaders so they can fulfill their call to leadership.

## Peter as the Servant Leader

Then finally, Peter evolves from the self-focused forceful leader to the servant leader in the author of the epistles of Peter, where he calls himself a fellow elder rather than the one in charge as he did in the past. In 1 Peter, a different Peter is seen than the one who was always first to speak with mixed results in the gospels. The story of Peter is a case study in transformation in his shift from a community disrupter to a community facilitator; he changed from a stumbling block to a building block (Tilstra, 2014). In 1 Peter 5, he begins to talk to the leaders as a fellow equal elder and he gives instructions to them in three contrasting statements while encouraging them to remember that as shepherds they will receive reward from the chief shepherd. He is pointing away from himself as the source of authority and leadership. In addition, there are several repetitions of inner texture in this section from verse 1 through verse 7. The repetitions include "elder," "glory," "shepherd," "flock," "humility," and "God." The focus here is on the concept of shepherd and their function with the flock, the followers. Then there is a focus on two seemingly opposite concepts of humility and glory.

The exhortation that begins the three sets of contrasts starts with the verb shepherd as a command. This is the mandate for these leaders to actively shepherd the flock or the people of God. This picture of shepherd leader looks back to the Old Testament where King David and other leaders in Israel are called shepherds. It is a picture of how to lead. It is also in imitation of the first Shepherd leader, the Lord Himself. Psalm 23:1 says the Lord is my shepherd and it goes on to describe the Lord's leadership to the psalmist as a shepherd. Leaders are to imitate God's leadership. The concept of shepherd as leader is traditional and it is applied to God and His leadership style as well as to various human leaders in the Old Testament (Witherington, 2007a). Then in the New Testament Jesus calls Himself the good shepherd in John 10. Leaders in the church are called shepherds, and as seen here, Jesus is called the chief shepherd. Jesus is following the Old Testament pattern of a shepherd leader where He sets the example for other leaders to follow and they set the example and pattern for others as Peter is doing here.

What does this shepherd leadership look like according to Peter? In this epistle, Peter is functioning as a wise pastor advising church leaders and he reflects the principles he learned under Jesus' mentorship and he is passing on what he learned to this next generation of leaders (Tilstra, 2014). Peter is the one who probably spent the most time with Jesus while He was on earth receiving instruction about leadership, though many times in the form of a rebuke or correction. Leaders today would be wise to heed his counsel.

Here in this section is a progressive texture where Peter gives three contrasts to help the leaders clearly understand how to lead. The first contrast is found in verse two. They are to shepherd by exercising oversight but not to do it under compulsion but willingly. This is speaking of the motive of the leader that the leader would shepherd not out of duty or duress but freely, openly with a good heart and attitude. The second contrast is lead with passion and zeal not for shameful gain, not just to make more money. Then the third gets to the heart of the matter. Do not lead by domineering others but be examples to them. Lead by being the role model as Jesus was for us and He still is as the chief shepherd. Table 6.1 shows these contrasts.

There is a reward and this reward is a crown of glory, Peter says he is going to participate in this glory as well. There is a reward for leading well; it is glory. Is this glory only for eternity or is there some aspect of this glory here on earth? The glory is a reward for those who lead well. One way that this word for "glory" can be translated is "honor." Will leaders who lead well eventually receive honor for leading this way. We are told by Paul to honor our leaders and to give double honor to those that lead well (1 Timothy 5:17). Leading well will bring honor in eternity but it can also bring honor here as well.

Then Peter changes the discussion to include all not just the elders, but it includes these elders. He then speaks of the crowning ingredient for leaders and followers, that of humility. Peter even explains why this is so important. It is because God gives grace—help and power—to the humble. In fact, this is so important that he explains how the person can humble themselves under God's hand. God helps with humility especially in difficult circumstances. Then the person, the leader, will be exalted if they walk in humility. It is important to understand humility. From the rich history of humility thought, humility is defined as a personal orientation founded on the willingness to see the self accurately and

**Table 6.1** Contrasts for shepherd leaders

| Shepherd | By exercising oversight | |
|---|---|---|
| Willingly | Not | Under compulsion |
| With zeal (eagerly) | Not | For gain |
| Example | Not | Domineering |

a propensity to put oneself in perspective; it involves neither self-abasement nor overly positive self-regard (Morris, Brotheridge, & Urbanski, 2005). It is not a low opinion of self but it is an accurate assessment, and in this place the leader sees the talents of others and the need for others as well.

Peter describes the shepherd leader as one who follows the chief shepherd and leads willingly, without a profit or gain mentality and as one who is not domineering. The essential quality is that of humility. He tells them to put on humility like clothing. It is not so much that it is external as it identifies who one is; it is the way one interacts with others based upon what has happened to the leader, as the leader has developed humility under God's hand, so it becomes apparent in all that the leader does in life and leadership. It is the most prominent thing others see in leaders—like clothing. These concepts confirm servant leadership but they also add new depth and nuance to the thinking about servant leadership in pressing deeply into the motives of the leader. Humility and being the example are clearly servant leadership issues but there is more here for consideration that will be examined later in this study.

## Instructions to Leaders

These instructions use this same picture of shepherd as seen in the Old Testament but now a further picture is added for contrast in the picture of a wolf and a lion. Servant leadership is taught in many different ways through the epistles of the New Testament as authored by Paul, James, and John. Paul talks about how wolves will come after the sheep once he is gone, in Acts 20. These wolves are false leaders. They lead for themselves and their own glory and appetites. According to Paul, in Acts 20:28–30, these wolves are leaders who will speak twisted things; actually, they will twist words to draw people after themselves. These are the antileaders who lead for their own glory and benefit. There are other analogies like this in the New Testament. One is the image of a lion, the arch enemy of sheep and shepherds in the natural realm. However, this picture is used as a spiritual analogy in 1 Peter 5 where the last section finished about sheep and shepherds.

In 1 Peter 5:8–11, the lion is a symbol of the devil who opposes the people. He tries to devour them with grief. The way this is seen in the world is through trouble and persecution. The elders to whom Peter spoke would understand this analogy of the lion and the shepherd and the sheep. They knew it was the shepherd's job to protect the sheep in this situation. However, to do so, they had to win the battle themselves. Sheep cannot fight lions; only a shepherd can, and if the shepherd fails all is lost for the sheep. The term that Peter uses here is the lion seeks to "devour." This term means to drink down and it is a picture of the destruction of the person (Davids, 1990).

In this short section, there are four repeated words from the inner texture of the pericope. These repeated words are "suffer," "firm," "God," and "grace." The issue here is suffering it as if a lion comes against the sheep, and it comes in the form of suffering. The answer is to resist him, the lion, by being firm. It does not say resist the suffering but resist the destruction that can come from suffering. People suffer in all kinds of ways and the tendency is to lose heart and become discouraged, to lose courage for life and mission. In Romans 5:1–5, Paul addresses this same issue but without the metaphor of the lion. He says we rejoice in sufferings. But the question to Paulis why should we rejoice in sufferings? Suffering produces perseverance according to Paul here in Romans. Now suffering can produce perseverance or if one responds incorrectly it produces the opposite—a lack of courage and bitterness. However, once it produces perseverance, this perseverance produces character and character, hope. So, the believer gets character development, which is part of the process of knowing God and it is important for effective, ethical leadership as well. How is the lion resisted? He is resisted by being firm in rejoicing and perseverance. Then once this happens (unknown time lapse inserted here) then God will restore, confirm, strengthen, and establish the person. These are similar words, but basically this person will not only be restored from discouragement but will also grow as a person and develop character. The leader must learn to win this battle first so that she/he can lead others through this same process. Here, the leader goes first to set the example and the pattern.

In servant leadership, there is the need for good character since it is a virtuous theory and virtues proceed from the person. This is an important component here. Possibly, in this text a way to help leaders develop character has been found. The way is not to add suffering to their lives. Instead, it is to teach them how to deal with present and future suffering then helping them redefine or live in a new way concerning their sufferings of the past. What happens when we are set free from troubles and pains and bruises of the past? New freedom, new power, and new vision happen and maybe even new motivations. Could dealing well with suffering become part of the training ground for leading, especially leading with a virtuous model of leadership? It is worth consideration and even inclusion in the foundation of a model of leadership.

## Servant Leadership in the Epistles

### Romans and Corinthians

The Roman and Corinthian correspondences give instructions for leaders both directly and indirectly about humility and the leader overcoming self-focus. Integral to Paul's concept of leadership were spiritual gifts that are discussed in Romans and Corinthians as well as in the Prison epistles, and this became Paul's way of describing how grace collectively operates in the community and this was central to Paul's thinking since he did not want grace to remain a mere doctrine but that it also functioned as a concrete reality for everyone (Choi, 2014). Here, grace functions as the divine gifting for the believer for different gifts for effective leadership. Gifts are the pieces of grace given to believers and to leaders. These are divine helps of grace or power from God to do the will of God. Christian leaders are empowered by God through grace to accomplish divine purpose. Yet it is not just here that Paul discusses leadership in connection to divine empowerment.

An important issue for Paul is that of character and even the development of character. In Romans, Paul connects suffering to perseverance and character. For Paul, character was not defined in human terms, such as personal traits, but entirely in relation to God, it was not from human nature but it was a gift from God given by the Spirit and it was measured by the image of Christ not a human measurement, yet it is in weakness and brokenness that we find the Christian leader, especially Paul presenting himself (Choi, 2014). There is an emphasis in these letters of gifting from God, yet a focus on character and character development through the process of weakness and even brokenness. The letters are literary windows into Paul's leadership where he goes to considerable lengths to demonstrate his leadership over these congregations and he defends his right to exercise leadership since these churches were founded by him and his coworkers or in the case of the Roman churches because he needs them for his mission to the Gentiles (Agosto, 2005). In these contexts, many different aspects of Paul's leadership are seen and explained sometimes directly and other times by implication. In these epistles, he explains concepts of leadership as he addresses the issues at hand in the churches. The question is how these aspects of Pauline leadership interact with the concepts of servant leadership.

Paul begins his Roman correspondence by positioning himself first as a servant of Christ but then he moves to his calling as an apostle or one sent on a mission and who had been set apart for a purpose. This calling was important in that it was the foundation from which he preached the good news and led the churches. Paul had not planted this church in Rome as he had many of the others that he led. Nevertheless, he established himself as a leader in this church based upon his calling to be an apostle. Here, the word "apostle" is a noun speaking of not just the position but also of the person. This call to be an apostle, a leader in the church, is not self-imposed but is a directive from the Lord and yet it is more than a position. Leadership begins in the mind of God as a gracious inclusion of humanity into the plans of God and yet God chooses people who do not seem to be the most qualified, perhaps because God considers calling as a continuous aspect of creation (Willimon, 2002). This calling to be an apostle was important to Paul not just in how he functioned but also in who he was as a person. God worked in him to establish His mission and gave him authority as a delegate to lead. The calling to lead is ontological in that it is not only a call to do but it is also a call to become someone more through internal development in the soul.

Then, toward the end of chapter 1 of Romans, Paul discusses how he is to lead the Roman believers in verses 8 through 15. This is a progressive texture in this pericope. He begins with "first" implying an ordered list with certain priorities in leading them. His first priority was to thank

God for them and for their faith. His focus was on the Romans and their connection to God. He encouraged them in their faith and how they had been faithful. His first step into leading the Romans was bringing a word of encouragement and yet that he was praying for them to continue in doing well. Then in the second place he wanted to see them to impart something to them so they would be strengthened. However, this was not to be a one-way connection from leader to follower in that Paul wanted it to be a mutual connection. Paul would impart to them but there would also be an impartation from them to Paul in the realm of encouragement. Here is seen an aspect of leader-follower connections that are more than top-down directives. In fact, these are not directives at all. These are growth connections for leader and follower. Third, Paul reveals how his calling is connected to the Roman church. In one sense, he is obligated to them as a result of His calling however; he is eager and willing to bring good news to them. This is paradoxical in that obligation and willing are seen as part of the same process. Usually, a person is considered to do something out of obligation or desire but here both are seen together. Paul is supposed to lead them but he leads by a much deeper desire than obligation. He is not only willing but eager, almost zealous about leading them.

Several concepts of leadership are found here in this interaction concerning Paul and his leadership for the Roman church. Paul's highest priority in leading them is to focus on them and bring encouragement to them. This leadership is follower centered. Paul then moves on to impart something to them, to serve them by equipping them for their spiritual lives. However, he stops here to include them as part of the process of leading and impartation in that he is to receive encouragement from them. There is a certain leadership reciprocity here. Finally, he connects his leadership to them to his calling. He is called to lead yet he leads them eagerly. This has to do with motive and why he leads them. Motive matters in leadership. His motive is his connection to and directive from the Lord but it is also in eagerness to serve them, the Roman Christians.

Returning to the concept of the internal issues of the leader, it is apparent that these issues like godly character must be developed. However, the immediate question comes to the forefront of how one develops internal issues of the soul. Behavioral issues are more easily developed like learning how to encourage others, but by themselves these external developments are not enough. Paul speaks directly to this issue in Romans 5:1–5.

Romans 5:1–4 begins with an argumentative texture with a modified form of the "if, then" argument. It begins with a since statement in that it has gone past "if" or guessing to a place of surety. Since the believer has been justified by faith then that person has peace with God. The condition has already been met of justification which brings peace. The result is now that the believer can rejoice in the present and coming glory of God. However, the purpose of the argument does not stop here. Paul goes on to contrast rejoicing in the glory of God and rejoicing in tribulation or trouble. The trouble with tribulation is that so many times it is totally misunderstood. Luther called this the hiddenness of God in that God many times hides Himself under opposites (Althaus, 1966). This paradox is the key to the development of godly character.

It is here that a progressive texture begins in this pericope. It begins with a simple statement that believers rejoice in sufferings or tribulation or pressures. Nevertheless, the first thought is to question that simple statement. As believers, is this what is actually done—rejoice in suffering? At first glance, this seems contradictory. However, in light of the rest of the progression, it becomes clear as to the intent and the purpose of the rejoicing. Following Paul's tight logic here through the progression gives insight for character development and even the source of love, which are both important qualities for biblical and servant leadership. It begins with rejoicing or even boasting in tribulation or suffering that comes from all kinds of situations. The reason for this rejoicing is that suffering produces perseverance. Paul says that suffering brings about perseverance (Romans 5:3). But how does it bring it about? There are several ways that a person can respond to suffering; but at the two ends of the spectrum of responses, there are two opposite possibilities. The first is bitterness. The book of Hebrews redefines suffering hardship as discipline from the Lord and in the exhortation in Hebrews 12:15 in responding to suffering it says that no one should come short of the grace of God and allow a root of bitterness to spring up. Many people respond to suffering through becoming bitter against God, life, a person, or people in general. Yet, the opposite and the way for grace is in perseverance. This may take some divine help in the soul but this is the place of grace. When the person responds to suffering with perseverance, character is produced. Character is the inner form that makes anyone or anything what it is—the essential "stuff" of the person, the inner reality—character determines behavior and behavior demonstrates character—it is deeper than philosophies (Guinness, 2003). This is not just character it is tried and approved character. Godly character is developed. The progression does not stop here, it goes on. This character brings about hope. This hope is a joyful and expectant hope of something future. In the earlier contrast in this text, this hope had a dualism to it of the glory of God both present and future. It is an expectation to see clearly the radiance of God in life now and in the future eternity. Here again we see a certain dualism. However, the hope here is in a different direction. This hope is directed toward God's work in us that will be fully manifest in eternity. Nevertheless, this love of God does not disappoint as it has already been poured out in the believer. The hope is the love of God in us and through us and it is already starting to work. The key to love is developing godly character. Love without character is a beginning, but love can only fully express itself through godly character since love is the ultimate in other orientation. Many get married with love without character and this makes it nearly impossible to follow through on the intent of love. Many want love but they do not know how to pay the price for love. The many broken marriages in our world testify to this reality. Many dream of love and write books and movies about love and about lost love. What about love found? When that love is found, many times it is destroyed by an inability to love well. The missing ingredient? Godly, mature character. For servant leadership to prosper, the leader must be able to love and this love must be developed through developing good, mature character.

In Romans 12:1–8, Paul addresses the issue of gifts implying that all have gifts and that part of service to God is the effective use of the gifts that are given. In connection to these gifts there is a scale that has been developed for job person fit using these gifts in Romans 12 as the basis for that fit for each individual (Della Vecchio & Winston, 2004). This study provides a background for the use of these gifts in leadership contexts. However, the point of this study is to move past that preliminary study and examine some specific issues for leadership generally and in the specific gift of leading. First is found the preparation for effective use of all the gifts in Romans 12:1–3. This section begins with argumentative texture. Since the believer lives under God's mercy, there are some results that should proceed from that state of grace. Then there are two contrasts and a statement of cause and effect. The first contrast is that the believers are to present their bodies but is an act of spiritual worship. Part of worship that is spiritual or unseen is done by the physical body that is seen. Presenting one's body to God is a surrender to serve the Lord in the way one lives and in effective use of the gifts that are given by Him. The second contrast is that the believer is not to be conformed to the world. The exhortation here is not to become a copy of the cultural and societal norms which are seen by actions but to be transformed. This transformation though does not begin in the external actions but in the internal issue of the soul in that of transformation. This transformation occurs through the renewing of the mind. This is a complete change of mind; this is a soul transformation that begins in the mind. This mind renewal is an internal process that could be related to the previous issue of character and love development. Where does the believer get this internal transformation? It is a work of the mind and soul connecting with Lord in knowing and growing in the understanding of the Lord through life and it comes from the experience of God in His Word and in His process of encounter. Then there is a result statement. This has a cause and effect relationship between the initial argument and the goal or the end result. The believer lives in these contrasts to be able to prove, test, and live out the will of God. The goal is to fully live the purpose of one's individual life.

Paul goes on to set the foundation for this purpose of living out divine purpose. There are two instructions by implication here. The first is that these gifts from God come with a warning. This is God at work in and through the individual but the person is to think soberly about this process. The key here is humility. Humility is to have an honest assessment of self. Remember, it is the Lord who gives grace. Humility is a key ingredient to full effectiveness in using gifts. They are gifts and can be used well but others are needed as well with their gifts. The second implication is that each is given with a measure. Some may have more of a measure than others. Remember in the giving of talents in the gospels. One received five talents, another two, and another one, and this was not the result of some previous activity; these talents were all simply given. The key to this parable is that they were judged by how they used their talents whether one or five. The thought is that the steward is responsible for faithfulness. Faithfulness is more than just showing up. This is what the one talent person thought. Faithfulness is increasing what has been given through use and development. Two issues then for effective use of the gift given are humility and faithfulness. Then Paul gives a very specific instruction to those who lead, to lead with diligence, to lead with genuine zeal and commitment. However, in this context are found separate gifts for serving and teaching as well. Does this mean that serving or even teaching is separate from leading? Can one person use several gifts? This could be a more detailed discussion for the future. However, for the present it appears that these gifts can be used in multiples; otherwise how could Paul teach and lead? If one cannot serve and lead then there would be a conflict in servant leadership. However, servant leading is seen in Jesus and others in Scripture. The way ahead is to hear the text for what it is saying about preparation and use of gifts in the different areas but particularly in the instruction to leaders.

The Paul that is met in 1 Corinthians has been a Christian for as long as 20 years, he is a mature believer and he is an apostle who has been engaged in missionary activities for more than a decade (Witherington, 1995). Paul speaks indirectly concerning leaders and leadership in 1 Corinthians 3 in a call for unity where there had been division. Some of the followers were saying they were of Apollos and others of Paul. In addressing this issue of division, Paul describes both him and Apollos as leaders. First, they were both servants as a general description of their leadership. The question here is whether Paul is referring to them as servants generally or as servants to the Lord. Then each leader has a different function though the goal is still the same to build the church in Corinth. Finally, Paul declares that both he and Apollos are workers or laborers together with God. However, the followers in the church are God's field or building. Both leaders and followers are partners with God but the picture of the goal of this process of leadership is growth. However, the growth is focused in the followers. Leaders here are described as servants who are part of a bigger enterprise with the goal of growth, but growth in the organization is growth in the followers.

In 1 Corinthians 12, Paul addresses the issue of spiritual gifts and how they are distributed to each person for the common good. Notice the purpose of these gifts; they are for the common good. For the good of the whole church, for the good of each member. The word here is to be profitable together, to be profitable for everyone together (Friberg & Friberg, 1994). It is for growth for all and not for the recipient of the gift but for those who receive the benefit of that gift through a person. In this way, spiritual gifts are unique in that they are not so much like Christmas gifts for the receiver, but they are given so others would benefit. This idea fits well into the worldview of servant leadership. Then, at the end of the chapter, Paul discusses a progressive list of gifts beginning first with apostles. According to Friberg and Friberg (1994), an apostle is a person who has the special task of founding and establishing churches. This person is a leader in the church and then, second, there are prophets, and, third, teachers. The further discussion at the end of chapter 12 indicates that that not everyone is one for these leaders but they have differing gifts for differing purposes. Nevertheless, there are some with these types of leader gifts. Yet, in the use of these gifts, there is a way to use them that is the best way as found in 1 Corinthians 13 and that way is love.

In Romans and Corinthians are found several themes for leadership that proceed from the issue of spiritual gifts and from the issue of Paul leading the church. In several places, Paul uses the term "servant" in describing leaders and their leadership. The implication is that these leaders are servants of the Lord rather than servants of others as was seen in the teachings of Jesus. However, when Paul describes this type of leadership, it includes a focus on others, a mutuality with others in leading, and a design for the growth of the individuals which is good for the group or the church or the called-out ones. Paul describes himself as an apostle who leads the church with care and yet as one who gives instruction. In these instructions are found some key elements for leadership, namely humility and faithfulness, as well as a paradoxical design for rejoicing in suffering. Paul develops some important ingredients for life and leadership in this context of suffering that produces perseverance, godly character, and hope, and then this becomes the foundation for effective love. In connection to spiritual gifts, love again is seen as the most effective way of leading and living. Concerning spiritual gifts, it is found that different gifts are given to different people and then the purpose of the gift is not for the person, even though the person is responsible to use the gift properly. The true recipients of the gifts are those that receive growth and help through the gift in that individual. Gifts by nature are intended to be other centered. In this discussion are seen several connections to servant leadership with a strong focus on others and bringing growth to others with a recognition for the need of character development in virtues like humility. Nevertheless, there are a few areas that need further exploration to nuance and expand servant leadership as in the area of dealing with suffering and perseverance.

## The Prison Epistles

In the Prison Epistles, Paul gives strong exhortations about theology, the Christian life, and how to lead using several pictures like that of a Roman guard. However, it is here that Paul gives a further perspective on the leadership of Christ as well as further details on spiritual gifts and leadership. In these epistles are found rich resources for the understanding of leadership from a biblical perspective.

In Ephesians 4:7–16, Paul returns to his theme of spiritual gifts but this time with a specific focus on leaders and leadership. This section begins with a premise and then develops with argumentative texture. The premise is that each person is given grace from Christ in a measure and this brings gifts to individuals. In this context, it is talking about gifts given to individuals who become leaders; it is the gift of leadership in different categories. The gifts listed here in Ephesians 4 involve leadership roles (Choi, 2014). However, in verse 11, the argument moves quickly to the purpose of these gifts of leadership concluding with results if the purpose is followed. There is an "if, then" implication though it is not clearly stated. Inside these later two sections of purpose and result, there are progressive textures that are related to each other with the idea of cause and effect. Paul uses the word "apostle" in the list of gifts in the broad sense concerning those who have been called by God to establish churches and the prophets are to edify and build the church (Arnold, 2010). These are leaders in the church but with different functions.

The purpose of these gifts and leadership ministries given to the church are first to equip the saints as the first stage in this first progressive texture. This is a process of adjustment that results in complete preparedness (Friberg & Friberg, 1994). Leaders are to equip and train the people of the organization or the church. The use of equipping here implies that some type of training went on and development of competency through practical training in line with giftedness (Choi, 2014). The purpose of this training is for the people to do the work of serving each other and encouraging or building others up. The Greek "work" here is the word for "service" (Friberg & Friberg, 1994). The focus goes from leader to follower and then from follower to others to build up and encourage others. This keeps processing until all become mature. So, what is the result of this leadership process? This moves into the second progressive texture. As a result, there will be maturity evidenced by stability, being able to speak truth, and love. Further in this progression every joint or member supplies or functions in their place bringing growth and walking in love. Christ has sovereignly endowed every individual with special abilities to serve others and it is the responsibility of the gifted leaders to equip others for a life of service with the goal of maturity and love for each other (Arnold, 2010). Leadership here is to serve others by training them to serve others with the focus on the followers becoming mature and able to interact with others in love. This has attributes of servant leadership but the focus is on the process of equipping followers to lead. While it begins with grace and gifts its result is love.

This pericope of Scripture in Philippians 2:5–11 exhorts the believers to the imitation of Jesus Christ in his self-emptying, but God exalted Him and He brings glory to the Father in the process. The highest example of a self-forgetful regard for the interest of others is portrayed by Christ, wherein believers have a perfect example of how they should behave in humility and self-renunciation (Muller, 1995). This hymn looks back to the exhortation to humility (2:1–4) and forward to the exhortation to obedience (2:12–18) with Christ exemplifying the qualities that Paul wants to see in the Philippians (Holloway, 2007). But how is this connected to leadership? Set in the first-century context of Philippi, the consensus is that this is a religious response to the tyranny of local Roman leadership and this opens the door for researchers to explore the hymn as an alternative, exemplary model of leadership rooted in a fir century, mimetic Christological spirituality (Bekker, 2007). There are several elements here to explore as a theological foundation upon which to build leadership thinking. This concept has to do with the pattern set by Jesus Christ, his nature and attitude, His obedience and humility, his motive and His goal of bringing glory to God, and his unique interaction with the Father. Paul is appealing to the Philippians not only to know about Christ but to be like Him and this form allows us to accurately reconstruct applications for leadership (Ayers, 2006).

Were these exhortations to believers generally or did they apply to leaders in Philippi? The letter itself was addressed to the saints as well as the overseers. However, this section, as seen previously, was a response to the Roman leadership. In context, Paul is communicating the realities of the nature of Jesus Christ by juxtaposing Jesus' humility to his position and power, two issues that are of unique concern to leaders (Ayers, 2006). Position and power, while important issues for leadership, are also concerns of the teachings of Jesus in the gospels. Jesus also uses the servant analogy, as seen here in Philippians, as an example and motivation of leadership in the gospels and this is also seen throughout the New Testament (Ayers, 2006). Paul presents Christ as a role model for others to imitate with two extreme measures, death and obedience; to humble Himself in stark contrast to emperors of Rome, Jesus willfully chose downward mobility as a path to exaltation (Gray, 2008). This model was one of intentional downward mobility as a path to leadership, not just of Rome but of every knee and tongue; so, how much more does this serve as a model for all lesser human forms of leadership? The servant model and humility are held up as ideals of leadership in the context of position and power in the Scripture with this passage in Philippians as an important example of this form of leadership.

This section in Philippians begins with the exhortation toward a proper attitude, an internal invisible issue but then moves to describe this attitude of Christ in a chiasm. The first point of the chiasm is that Christ is God (verses 5–6a), the second is that He descended to earth and became a servant (6b–7), then, the third and central focus of the chiasm is that he became obedient to the death on the cross (8), then, the first counterpoint is that Jesus ascended and became exalted (9), and the second counterpoint

owledged as God (10–11) (Bekker, 2007). This structure
)edience and death of Christ, not as the redemptive act
iry act to be followed, not the death but the obedience.
rist as an example, Paul wants the Philippians to imitate
put the interests of others first and willing to give up
___ p.......ege and status that was his as God (Grudem, 1994). It is
preceded by humbling himself and followed by divine exaltation and
bringing glory to God. This is the general process of leadership, it begins
with a proper attitude that produces humility that results in God exalting
or empowering the leader and bringing glory to God.

This concept of leadership begins ontologically with the leader becoming a servant through a formation process that begins with self-emptying
to receive the formation of the Lord, especially in the internal areas concerning character and destiny. Then from this ontological reality comes
the change in the leader operating in humility and obedience; this comes
from the ontological reality of this person who has taken on the form of
a servant. The leader takes on a process of bearing the image of Christ and
leading others into this process. The goal of this process is to bring honor
to God, bringing further revelation of God. In addition, a special relationship is developed with God. These elements then become the foundation issues for an effective leader, not only in leading the church but
also in leading the believers to become effective disciples of Christ and a
viable Christian community. In the gospels are seen the teachings and
actions of Jesus concerning leadership but here in this epistle is found the
explanation of Jesus' servant leadership. There is an alignment here with
the model of servant leadership in the leader becoming a servant.
However, this concept further nuances the model with the internal work
of self-emptying and the goal of bringing glory to God. In addition, this
idea shows that the leader will actually receive benefit from this process as
well. This text will be further examined later in this study.

In both pericopes, there are areas that confirm and even nuance servant leadership as in Ephesians that focuses on the follower and on
training the follower to serve. Then in Philippians the focus is on serving others but through the foundation of godly character. Nevertheless,
in both sections, there are areas that can expand or further nuance servant leadership with the Ephesian focus on the process toward maturity

in the follower and the result of love. Then in Philippians the concept goes past serving to the ontological issues of becoming a servant by self-emptying.

## The Pastoral Epistles

Then Paul becomes emphatic in the Pastoral Epistles about the leader being blameless and showing good fruit through relationships. These are issues that need careful consideration in the context of servant leadership and they even extend beyond servant leadership. It is here that Paul gives particular insight for leaders and leadership with implications for leadership development from a New Testament perspective. It is here that the instructions about leaders become very explicit and detailed calling for a detailed examination.

In I Timothy, Paul is giving Timothy personal instruction and encouragement in faithfully carrying out his task of leading the church in Ephesus (Zehr, 2010). This instruction gives insight for leadership from a biblical perspective. The opening formula, "Here is a trustworthy saying," draws strong attention to the importance of the overseer's office, it is a way of bringing out the dignity of the office before introducing the qualifications required (Guthrie, 1999). This is an important issue for church leadership for Paul in the Ephesians context. This need for qualified church leaders reflects the need of Ephesus, and there can be insight gleaned from Paul's instruction to Timothy; though the cultural context is different, the human context is very much the same.

In the inner texture of the text, there is both a repetitive and a progressive texture pattern. There are five sets of words that are repeated in this text; "overseer" is repeated two times, "must" is repeated three times, "not" is repeated four times, "fall" two times, and "devil" two times. These help to form significant thoughts in the understanding of this trustworthy statement about church leaders. In that, there are certain *must* issues for leaders as well as negations; there are certain qualities needed as well as certain things that are not true about these leaders. Additionally, in the end it is the devil that will oppose these leaders, not just circumstances or other people. Though many of the *musts* and *nots* are natural issues, it is a spiritual task with spiritual applications to lead the church. The purpose for these natural qualities is not only to set the example for others but is also to persevere in proper effective leadership. This is so that the leader "will not fall" is the refrain in the last two verses of this section. The repetition of the *musts* and *nots* set up positive and negative issues for leadership qualifications here in this leadership description.

However, before the list can be made it must be noted that there is a progressive texture as well that is deeply embedded in the text. The first progression moves from the desire of the person to be an overseer, to characteristics that must be in the person, to something outside of the person that he/she must have. Then there is a progression of the location of the leadership from office in verse 1 to the household in verse 4, to the church in verse 5, then to outside the church in verse 7. In addition, there is a progression of the actions, from work in verse 1 to manage in verse 4, to take care of in verse 5, to having a good reputation in verse 7. This texture sets up a sequence or progression for a framework in which to understand these qualifications.

There is also a further inner texture in an opening-middle-closing texture. Opening-middle-closing texture resides in the nature of a beginning, body, and conclusion of a section of discourse (Robbins, 1996). This section, though not narrative, is a discourse from Paul to Timothy on church leadership for Ephesus. The section begins with discussion about the overseer, then moves to the qualifications of the overseer, and concludes with a discussion of how the leader is to overcome the devil. The repetitive, progressive, and opening-middle-closing texture can be seen graphically (Table 6.2).

According to the inner texture of the text, it divides into four sections with each focusing on different actions and qualifications for the leader. Asake (1998) synthesizes these qualifications under four categories: personal qualifications, family qualifications, public qualifications, and ministry qualifications. Though these categories are similar, they are not topical; instead, they relate to and draw from the different sections of this pericope. There are four sections, but when viewed according to the texture of this pericope, they reveal new insights.

The first set of qualifications has to do with the office and the work of the leader. The one who desires this position, there is a certain amount of

**Table 6.2** The inner texture of I Timothy 3:1–7

| I Timothy 3:1–7 repetition and Opening-middle-closing pattern | | | | | Progressive pattern | | |
|---|---|---|---|---|---|---|---|
| | | | | | Person | Location | Actions |
| 3:1 | Overseer | | | | Desire | Office | Work |
| 3:2 | Overseer | Must | | | Must be | | |
| 3:3 | | | Not | | | | |
| 3:4 | | Must | | | Must be | Household | Manage |
| 3:5 | | | Not | | | Church | Take care of |
| 3:6 | | | Not | Fall Devil | | | |
| 3:7 | | Must | Not | Fall Devil | Must have | Outside the church | Good reputation |

work affiliated with it, but one must become a certain kind of person to be able to properly do the work, this has to do with character. Character is the inner form that makes anyone or anything what it is. It is the inner reality in which thoughts, speech and behavior are rooted (Guinness, 2003). This is not a list of things to do as much as what one must become as a person. Leadership is about leading by example, or modeling, one leads more by who they are than by what is said.

The first set of qualifications has ten positive qualifications and two negative ones. It also involves ten internal issues and two external issues that can be seen by others. It begins with the attribute of being above reproach, having unquestionable integrity (Conner, 1989), or not only of good report but deservedly so (Guthrie, 1999). Zehr (2010) declares that this virtue covers the whole list in a general way. It appears though that this virtue is a general statement about the first section in this pericope with its focus on internal character issues with some external issues that can be seen.

How is the leader to be above reproach? By being the husband of one wife, some have thought this to forbid second marriages after divorce (Guthrie, 1999), while others declare that it does not involve divorce and/or remarriage but excludes immoral behavior (Conner, 1989). Certainly, this calls for fidelity and integrity to the marriage covenant and this is an important ingredient to the leader's credibility (Zehr, 2010). Being above reproach involves fidelity to the marriage covenant, which is an attribute that is internal concerning intent, but it can also be seen by those inside and outside of the church.

The next three virtues are related and they describe an orderly life, temperate, prudent, and respectable (Guthrie, 1999). The first two virtues call attention to inner character while the third speaks of one's external deportment, and this shows that the leader has to be well mannered and orderly (Zehr, 2010). According to I Timothy 3:2, a leader must be honorable and not boastful, have a sound mind, and watchful, not careless (Conner, 1989). These inner qualities involve self-control as well as having a disciplined mind in the living of a life that is honorable and not arrogant.

The next two qualities in this first section for the work of a leader have to do with ministry as a leader in the church. Hospitality would be particularly important in the early church since without it expansion of the church would be seriously retarded (Guthrie, 1999). The ability to teach, though not a character trait, was an important skill since the leader was responsible to instruct the believers in the truth of God's word (Zehr, 2010). The word "teacher" here is instructor, one who is accorded status and may be used as a term of respect (Nyland, 2010). It is important that these ministry skills are found in the midst of character qualities without which these skills could become counterproductive. This is not simply an arbitrary list but it is four sets of ministry qualifications that cannot be arbitrarily dismissed or divided for convenience into topical directives for the Western mind. They are clusters of qualities that center on the work of the leader, managing as a director of the household, caring as a church leader, and facing the challenges from outside the church as an effective leader. The Western mind's propensity to make lists from dialogue stripping it from its context is clearly seen in the lists for leadership made from this pericope.

The next five issues are set in opposition to each other not just positive and negative qualities on a list. Nyland (2010) translates this text as someone who is not a drunk or gets into fist fights but who is fair, peaceful, and free from greed. This is a character quality of integrity and wholeness. A leader is an emotionally healthy person with confidence in the gospel message and in himself because an impatient leader could easily hand out rough treatment to an immature believer (Zehr, 2010). This is about the leader's internal character qualities that induce him to handle difficult situations in a godly manner. It is not primarily about wine or money; it is about the state of the person's soul that manifests in times of stress and pressure.

The second section in this text concerns the management of the household. The word "manage" carries the sense of presiding over activities in an official capacity and is used in the context of one who is a leader, supervisor or director, the word encompasses care, concern, and official rule with authority (Nyland, 2010). Any man unable to govern his children graciously by maintaining good discipline is not able to govern in the church (Guthrie, 1999). The leader must manage his family well as a ground upon which to build good management of the household of God. Implementing care and concern with authority is an extremely difficult task and the family is the training ground for this artful ability to govern. It has to do with the ability and the character of the person leading and it must be practiced first in the home before it is practiced in the organization.

The third section builds upon the first two sections; these qualities cannot be separated but are interrelated. This third section deals with taking care of the church of God. This is an important task that cannot be done by a novice. The leader cannot be newly planted in the community because his/her head can swell and he/she can become conceited, literally his/her head is filled with smoke, and without the benefit of a mature mind he/she can fall under the same condemnation as the devil (Zehr, 2010). The same condemnation as the devil, this is judgment for the sin of pride, since the devil became conceited and when he lifted himself up God threw him down. The more natural interpretation is judgment meted out for the sin of pride (Guthrie, 1999). Not only are there character qualities necessary for this type of leadership but also the ultimate test is that of humility. Can this person resist the pride that will come from being a leader? This is the ultimate question since this is extremely important in the life of the person, the leader, and it is important in leading the church or any organization.

The fourth section involves the leader's reputation with those outside of the church and brings him/her into direct conflict with the devil. In the previous section, there was a need not to fall under the same condemnation as the devil, not follow his ways. This section involves not falling into the snare set by the devil in direct confrontation. Unethical and unwise conduct can easily disgrace a leader and become a snare of the devil who seeks to slander the church through the non-Christian community (Zehr, 2010). The word used here for snare was used to refer to the wooden horse of Troy and refers to a trick in the form of a trap that will hold one fast (Nyland, 2010). This trap is a strategy of the devil to bring reproach, or a bad reputation not only to the leader but to the church and to the gospel itself because of the weaknesses in the leader. The ability to be above reproach is the culmination of the previous character qualities in the foundation of leadership for the leader.

The process of leadership begins with the person desiring the office and thereby developing qualities of self-control and integrity that are manifest in the marriage and in peacefulness which are necessary for this office. The qualifications continue in the household as the leader manages his/her household in learning to use authority with care, as manifest in the family and children. However, the leader cannot be a new convert and must develop the quality of humility to properly take care of or lead the church. Finally, the leader must maintain a good reputation even outside the church to actively overcome the strategies set against the church to discredit the gospel and to develop proper strategies for the advance of the gospel. This is a result of the culmination of the qualities needed for leadership including personal maturity (Fig. 6.1).

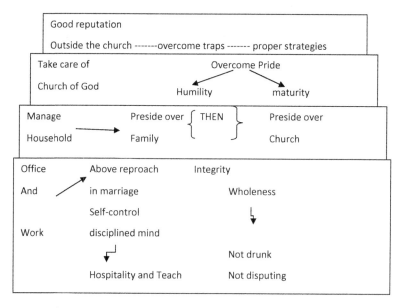

**Fig. 6.1** Biblical model of leadership from 1 Timothy 3:1–7

This concept of leadership is focused on internal character qualities but ones that manifest in certain important behaviors that can be seen and are part of effective leadership. This model is internally driven and has many connections to servant leadership. Some of these qualities would include humility and personal maturity with character qualities like integrity. However, it also takes into account qualities to overcome inevitable opposition and pressure that comes with leadership. This model is internally driven by character development that is manifest in behavior while being concerned with issues of maturity, humility, and a good reputation. The design is to become an effective leader to be able to be effective in teaching, hospitality, proper strategy, and overcoming opposition. These qualities are effective because they are built upon the internal godly character qualities. The overarching issue here is the internal character of the leader in being blameless. Nevertheless, there are some extensions past servant leadership that could facilitate virtue development for servant leadership. These extensions would include the issues of wholeness and self-control. In addition, there may be some places that this concept moves beyond servant leadership in areas of managing or presiding and learning to be above reproach as well as developing effective strategies for overcoming problems and for future growth.

## The General Epistles

John focuses on love in leadership which is an important component of servant leadership and James focuses on compassion. However, other epistles give glimpses or windows into the New Testament concepts of leadership with short directives sometimes aimed at instructing followers and other times aimed at instructing leaders.

In Hebrews 13:7, the author gives an exhortation to the followers to remember their leaders with particular considerations. These considerations for followers then become a picture of leadership from the perspective of the leader being the one to speak the word of God and the model to follow. The essence of ancient education was following good models or imitating them (Witherington, 2007b). This understanding and process is implied in this text. This verse has a progressive texture with three steps in following their leaders. First, the followers are to call to mind the leader and the word of God spoken to them. Leaders need to have an ability to speak the word from God, to give insight and directives. The gifts in Ephesians 4 all concern leadership roles involving mostly speech (Choi, 2014). Leadership involves communication and here it is communication from the word of God. Then the follower is to consider the outcome of the leader's way of life. The successful outcome of their behavior or way of life is to be imitated (Witherington, 2007b). Leadership involves living an exemplary life for others to follow, the leader is to be a role model but not just in organizational life but also in his/her personal life. Finally, the follower is to imitate the faith and the faithfulness of the leader. The Christian leader is to have a vibrant faith that can be imitated. In this context, leadership involves communication, with a role model life and faith. These issues can impact servant leadership yet they seem to be outside the normal parameters of the contemporary models.

In 1 Peter 5:1–6, Peter gives explicit instructions to the elders in the church on how they should lead. He addresses the elders by identifying himself as a fellow elder while not using the term "apostle" and this is the only place in the New Testament that this term is used (Shepherd, 2014). He continues by calling himself a witness of the sufferings of Christ and a partaker of the glory to follow. He does not use titles as much as descriptors of who he is and how he is one of them, the elders of the church. Peter refused special privilege here locating himself as an elder alongside other elders (Greene, 2007). He then quickly moves to a simple instruction for the leaders in how they should lead. However, he then moves to a progressive texture of contrasts to explain how this leading should be done and he talks about the reward of leadership but then with a final exhortation to humility.

He begins the exhortation with the simple command to shepherd the flock of God. This is reminiscent of the final exhortation that Jesus gave to Peter on the shore of Galilee in John 21. Jesus asked Peter if he loved Him and Peter said he did to which Jesus responded with the command to feed His sheep. Peter here uses the same verb of shepherd as Jesus used when He told Peter to tend His sheep (Grudem, 1999). Peter passed on this instruction to these newer leaders in the church. The imperative form of the verb is used here (Laniak, 2006). In other words, this was a command. It was not just instructions on how to do this way of leading, but it was intended as a command to be able to lead effectively, to lead biblically. The concept of shepherd as applied to leaders among God's people is traditional and it is applied to God and God's leadership style as well as to human leaders in the Old Testament (Witherington, 2007a). This concept was familiar to the people of the first century, yet it was continually being updated by Jesus and now by Peter. He then unpacks this concept with three progressive contrasts of shepherd leadership. To be an effective elder or leader and to shepherd or tend or lead the flock well, it must be done a certain way. Contrasting usually helps to clarify an issue when the opposite is seen; it makes the issue clearer. Peter's goal here is to be very clear about how to be an effective, godly leader in the imitation of Jesus since He is the chief shepherd. The first set of three contrasts sets willingness against compulsion in the oversight of the flock. The leader was to be the shepherd over the flock eagerly or spontaneously not under compulsion (Witherington, 2007a). This is an issue of internal motivation, it answers the question of why one leads. The second contrast sets the issue of personal gain against a desire to give. Leadership was not to be motivated by greed for financial gain by eagerness to serve others with a desire to give (Jobes, 2005). The second issue deals with focus that is either a self-focus or other focus. The final contrast sets dominance in leadership against leading by example. This paints a picture of the contrast in shepherding between a shepherd who drives the sheep by commands or the shepherd who leads the sheep by calling them by name like Jesus who said that He knew His sheep. This was not a hierarchical exercise of power but a horizontal demonstration by example (Elliot, 2000). This final contrast deals with the issue of how to use power, it was to be used with the leader becoming the example rather than used to control and command. These three contrasts show the way to shepherd against the backdrop of human tendencies in leading. It is a contrast between positive and negative leadership qualities. The three concepts on the negative side carry the sense of personal gain and domination, while qualities on the positive side are other centered focused on serving and forgetful of personal advantage (Shepherd, 2014). The issues of leadership here are deeper issues of the soul concerning motive, focus, and even learning to use power properly.

All of this talk of shepherding and now Peter turns the discussion to the Chief Shepherd, Jesus. He is the ultimate Shepherd leader and this discussion has been an extension of how to be a shepherd leader that begins in the Old Testament where it is found that "The Lord is my Shepherd" (Psalm 23:1). Then Jesus declares Himself to be the good shepherd (John 10) and gives instruction to Peter on how to shepherd the flock (John 21). This continues this discussion with specific instruction about how to be a good shepherd leader. However, the discussion does not stop here. It continues with a promise of reward. This could disturb some people especially in light of the other focus of the previous discussion. Nevertheless, there is a reward for good leading. This reward is a crown of glory. Notice though this is a result not a motive for leading. There is a reward to other focus but it is not counter to this other-centered leading. Yet, this is not the final word that Peter has for leaders. The final word is for all including leaders. It is an exhortation to humility. This is of supreme importance whether a follower or a leader. God gives grace to the humble and the instruction to each individual is to humble themselves. In reality, if this is not done God will take special care to bring humility. Humility is the core ingredient for these other issues. Humble yourselves … so that at the proper time He may exalt you (1 Peter 5:6). God will help the leader come to the right place at the right time. Humility then is the key foundation for coming to a place of usefulness. In this exhortation, there are several connections with servant leadership including humility and an emphasis on other focus. However, these concepts for leadership dive deeply into the soul of the leader impacting motive and even the use of power that are not addressed in the current models of servant leadership.

## Apocalyptic Servant Leadership

Then there is the leader in the apocalyptic context that must lead by serving others with the message of reality, not that the world is ending but that the world is the place that is lived until the end and in light of that one must lead to help others and bring glory to God. In Revelation 1, John is seen as the servant who sees the revelation of Jesus Christ. This message is sent to show the servants of the Lord the things that must happen. Then John as the servant brings this message to the other servants. There are two things to notice here. The first is that all to whom this text is written are considered servants. The second is that John is also considered a servant or a servant to the Lord and yet he is a servant to the servants as well. How does he serve them? He serves them by bringing a message of instruction and yet of hope in the midst of dark days of persecution. Those that are servants of the Lord usually become servant to others. However, there is a further issue here in that John as a servant brings words of hope and help in the midst of turmoil. This is a further nuance to the function of servant leadership in bringing a message of courage and hope, especially in times of turmoil and uncertainty.

## Other Leadership Issues and Models in the New Testament

There are other models and concepts of leadership that are taught in the text of the New Testament. Some of these models would include transformational and authentic leadership. In addition, there are concepts for leadership that do not fit any present models. For example, Jesus was a servant leader but he was also a transformational leader. His leadership easily fits into the overall structure of transformational leadership. Jesus was effective in inspirational motivation, He cast a vision for making disciples of all nations and millions, billions of people have caught and participated in that vision through the ages of the church. Jesus was the ultimate leader in using idealized influence in that He is the ultimate example to follow. Peter tells us we are to follow in His exact steps. It is this imitation of Christ that sets the bar not only for leadership but also for life for the believer. As far as intellectual stimulation, he was always challenging and pushing on with new ideas. He used formulas like "it is written, but I say to you." Finally, He was the ultimate in individualized consideration. Though He spent time with crowds, He spent more times with His disciples and even individuals like unnamed people who were sick or troubled. He had many individualized conversations with people who He helped and He was not as interested in those with power unless of course they needed His help. Add to this the concept of authentic leadership. This is a developed theory but at its core it has to do with authenticity and it was established as a response to corruption in leadership in the twenty-first century. Jesus was the ultimate in opposing and overcoming corruption while being highly authentic even when others, including His disciples, did not understand Him. Add to this list some of the issues that have been found in this study in areas of motive and character that are not addressed in contemporary models of leadership. This list of leadership concepts in the New Testament is quite extensive. The question is whether these concepts can be brought together for a cohesive concept for biblical leadership.

## Leadership Lessons from the New Testament

So what is to be done with these New Testament issues of leadership? The leadership lessons from the New Testament are broad and very profound. Many of these lessons include a deeper understanding of issues like humility, love and compassion. Other lessons include the way to becoming a servant that is ontological, it is part of who one is and the path is both countercultural and counterintuitive. In addition, the leader will serve people and God by bringing glory to God. The teleology of leadership is to show the real God to others and with compassion help them to fulfill the divine purpose given to them. Finally, there are issues of problem solving, strategy, and even vision for the mission seen in these texts concerning leadership. This helps in the development of a biblical servant leadership. However, in some ways this moves beyond servant leadership.

In these texts are found issues of success and failure in leadership. One of the causes of these failures is what could be termed as the dark side of leadership. Concerning the negative aspects of leadership narcissism or narcissistic leadership has been an important area of research recently. Schmidt (2008) has declared that there is a unique construct of dysfunctional leadership called toxic leadership and he has developed a scale for this type of leadership and narcissistic leadership is a component of this toxic leadership. In addition, Conger (1989) investigated what he called the dark side of charismatic leadership. Though he saw negative effects of this leadership, he saw it as unintentional. However, this began to bring to the forefront the need to study some of these negative aspects of leadership even when the leadership was effective in some ways. In the Western worldview, the zeal for pragmatism has tempted society to believe that if something works it is good and all of its parts are good. This North American fascination with function has mesmerized us into a heresy of pragmatism. This thinking can be challenged on several levels and should at least be tested when it comes to the issue of leadership.

Narcissism is a personality trait encompassing grandiosity, arrogance, self-absorption, entitlement, fragile self-esteem, and hostility; yet, it is an attribute of many powerful leaders. Narcissistic leaders have grandiose belief systems and leadership styles and are generally motivated by their needs for power and admiration rather than empathetic concern for the constituents and institutions they lead. However, narcissists also possess the charisma and grand vision that are vital to effective leadership (Rosenthal & Pittinsky, 2006). This concept of leading is directly opposed to servant leadership. Yet, does this mean that servant leaders are immune to this human tendency especially in the light of success? Narcissistic leadership occurs when leaders' actions are principally motivated by their own egomaniacal needs and beliefs, superseding the needs and interests of the constituents and institutions they lead (Rosenthal & Pittinsky, 2006). This is the very opposite of servant leadership and in essence a call for very serious consideration and further development of the model of servant leadership since so many leaders have followed the path of this dark side of leadership.

The issue of power and leadership is historic and controversial. Machiavelli (A.D. 1469–1527) is one of the best-known political theorists of all time whose position was that leaders are essentially selfish, self-interested, and self-protective and his concept of politics involved power relations, divorcing politics from virtue in the name of realism (Guinness, 2000). His concept of leadership was that power was to be used for the advancement of the leader. A good leader, according to Machiavelli, would consider self first and even use deception as a tool of power.

Despite the positive features in many theories of leadership, there are some weaknesses including a bias toward heroic concepts of leadership and a lack of sufficient specification of underlying influence processes

(Yukl, 2012). Can this heroic leadership concept become a problem as the leader becomes more powerful and the followers more enamored with the leader? As contemporary leaders become more compulsively attuned to polling and focus groups, leadership becomes codependent on followership and the public with the result of mediocre leadership, reinforced by trends toward the cult of personality and celebrity (Guinness, 2000). This trend toward personality and celebrity though effective in some ways has some further weaknesses. These weaknesses can be overcome by servant leadership especially as this model is seen in the New Testament with internal character development as a foundation for leadership. This speaks to a weakness in some models of leadership in the lack of specifications of the underlying influence processes. It is not only a question of how the leader motivates the followers but it is also a question of the internal motivation or processes within the leader. This is addressed in the context of the biblical teachings on good leadership. However, this brings us back to the definition of Narcissistic leadership having to do with the internal needs of the leader in a grandiose sense of self-importance, preoccupation with success and power, excessive need for admiration, entitlement, lack of empathy, envy, inferiority, and hypersensitivity. These are internal issues and if left unchecked they can grow into self-issues that bring disaster to the leader and others. Effective leadership can suffer from a "heroic leadership" bias and it has the potential to be abused. This abuse can relate to power, manipulation, and it can be used for destructive purposes. Part of the problem is that many of the models of leadership look only at behaviors and external measures of success. These models do not equip the leader with the proper tools for addressing the allure of power when the models of leadership succeed.

The way forward for leadership is not just the question of effectiveness but it is the question of motive and internal issues. Though many models are effective, they can come with a high cost of individual and organizational destruction. The way forward includes a further development of the biblical model as found in these texts in the New Testament as the foundation and the focus of leadership. Then possibly a new model could be developed by carefully examining some of the characteristics of effective models of leadership, particularly servant leadership. But this must be done carefully to not lose the focus of biblical leadership. This is not an appeal for a return to tradition. It is an appeal to view leadership with eyes wide open and to reexamine the biblical model where there is more insight for leadership for the present and the future.

## Conclusion

Many pericopes have been examined here in the discussion of biblical servant leadership. In this search, there have been many discoveries of further nuances and explanations or even expansions for servant leadership. In addition, some of the leadership concepts have moved beyond servant leadership. However, the question is whether this movement beyond servant leadership is a critique of this model or whether it is a place for further research and expansion. The problem and the area for further discussion is how to take all of these various elements and bring them together into a model of biblical servant leadership or should they be pursued as simply biblical leadership. Can these issues be brought together under one heading or are they simply different tools in the leader toolbox to be used when needed? This is an important question. At the very least, this study has shown the diversity and complexity of leadership issues as found in the New Testament. Now the issue is to understand them as they interact together to form a way of leading that is fully biblical.

## References

Agosto, E. (2005). *Servant Leadership: Jesus & Paul*. St. Louis, MO: Chalice Press.

Althaus, P. (1966). *The Theology of Martin Luther*. Minneapolis, MN: Fortress Press.

Arnold, C. (2010). *Ephesians (Zondervan Exegetical Commentary on the New Testament)*. Grand Rapids, MI: Zondervan.

Asake, M. N. (1998). *An Exposition of 1 Timothy 3:1–7 and Titus 1:5–9 with Application to Bajju ECWA Churches in Northern Nigeria*. Unpublished dissertation, Dallas Theological Seminary, Dallas, TX.

Ayers, M. (2006). Towards a Theology of Leadership. *Journal of Biblical Perspectives in Leadership, 1*, 3–27.

Bekker, C. J. (2007). *Sharing the Incarnation: Towards a Model of Mimetic Christological Leadership.* Paper presented at the Biblical Perspective Research Roundtable.

Burns, J., Shoup, J., & Simmons, D. (Eds.). (2014). *Organizational Leadership: Foundations and Practices for Christians.* Downers Grove, IL: InterVarsity Press.

Choi, P. R. (2014). The Pauline Epistles. In S. Bell (Ed.), *Servants and Friends: A Biblical Theology of Leadership* (pp. 291–307). Berrien Springs, MI: Andrews University Press.

Conger, J. A. (1989). *The Charismatic Leader: Behind the Mystique of Exceptional Leadership.* San Francisco, CA: Jossey-Bass.

Conner, K. J. (1989). *The Church in the New Testament.* Chichester, UK: Sovereign World Ltd.

Davids, P. H. (1990). *The First Epistle of Peter: New International Commentary on the New Testament.* Grand Rapids, MI: William B. Eerdmans.

Della Vecchio, D., & Winston, B. E. (2004). *A Seven-Scale Instrument to Measure the Romans 12 Motivational Gifts and a Proposition that the Romans 12 Gift Profiles Might Apply to Person-Job Fit Analysis.* Virginia Beach, VA: School of Leadership Studies, Regent University.

Elliot, J. H. (2000). *The Anchor Bible: 1 Peter.* New Haven, CT: Yale University Press.

Friberg, T., & Friberg, B. (1994). *Analytical Greek New Testament (GNM)* (2nd ed.). n.p.: Timothy and Barbara Friberg.

Gray, D. R. (2008). Christological Hymn: The Leadership Paradox of Philippians 2:5–11. *Journal of Biblical Perspectives in Leadership, 2*(1), 3–18.

Greene, J. (2007). *1 Peter: Two Horizons New Testament Commentary.* Grand Rapids, MI: William B. Eerdmans.

Grudem, W. (1994). *Systematic Theology.* Grand Rapids, MI: Zondervan Publishing House.

Grudem, W. (1999). *The First Epistle of Peter: An Introduction and Commentary.* Grand Rapids, MI: William B. Eerdmans Publishing Company.

Guinness, O. (2000). *When No One Sees: The Importance of Character in an Age of Image.* Colorado Springs, CO: NavPress.

Guinness, O. (2003). *The Call: Finding and Fulfilling the Central Purpose of Your Life.* Nashville, TN: W Publishing.

Guthrie, D. (1999). *The Pastoral Epistles* (Vol. 14, 2nd ed.). Grand Rapids, MI: Wm. B. Eerdmans Publishing Company.

Holloway, P. A. (2007). *Consolation in Philippians: Philosophical Sources and Rhetorical Strategy, Society for New Testament Studies Monograph Series*. New York, NY: Cambridge University Press.

Jobes, K. (2005). *1 Peter: Baker Exegetical Commentary on the New Testament*. Grand Rapids, MI: Baker Academic.

Laniak, T. S. (2006). *Shepherds After My Own Heart: Pastoral Traditions and Leadership in the Bible*. Downers Grove, IL: InterVarsity Press.

Morris, A. J., Brotheridge, C. M., & Urbanski, J. C. (2005). Bringing Humility to Leadership: Antecedents and Consequences of Leader Humility. *Human Relations, 58*(10), 1323–1350.

Muller, J. J. (1995). *The Epistles of Paul to the Philippians and Philemon*. Grand Rapids, MI: Wm. B Eerman's Publishing Company.

Nyland, A. (2010). *Pastoral Epistles: The Source New Testament: With Extensive Notes on Greek Word Meaning*. Australia: Smith and Sterling Publishing.

Robbins, V. K. (1996). *Exploring the Texture of Texts: A Guide to Socio-Rhetorical Interpretation*. Harrisburg, PA: Trinity Press International.

Rosenthal, S. A., & Pittinsky, T. L. (2006). Narcissistic Leadership. *Leadership Quarterly, 17*(6), 617–633.

Sauvagnat, B. J. (2014). Barnabas: A Study in Empowering Leadership. In S. Bell (Ed.), *Servants and Friends: A Biblical Theology of Leadership* (pp. 323–337). Berrien Springs, MI: Andrews University Press.

Schmidt, A. A. (2008). *Development and Validation of the Toxic Leadership Scale*. University of Maryland.

Shepherd, T. R. (2014). The General Epistles. In S. Bell (Ed.), *Servants and Friends: A Biblical Theology of Leadership* (pp. 211–226). Berrien Springs, MI: Andrews University Press.

Tilstra, D. (2014). Peter: A Narrative of Transformation. In S. Bell (Ed.), *Servants and Friends: A Biblical Theology of Leadership* (pp. 291–307). Berrien Springs, MI: Andrews University Press.

Willimon, W. H. (2002). Back to the Burning Bush. *Christian Century, 119*(9), 7.

Witherington, B. (1995). *Conflict and Community in Corinth: A Socio-Rhetorical Commentary on 1 and 2 Corinthians*. Grand Rapids, MI: W.B. Eerdmans.

Witherington, B. (2007a). *Letter and Homilies for Hellenized Christians: A Socio-Rhetorical Commentary on 1–2 Peter*. Downers Grove, IL: InterVarsity Press.

Witheringon, B. (2007b). *Letter and Homilies for Hellenized Christians: A Socio-Rhetorical Commentary on Hebrews, James and Jude.* Downers Grove, IL: InterVarsity Press.

Yukl, G. A. (2012). *Leadership in Organizations.* Englewood Cliffs, NJ: Prentice-Hall.

Zehr, P. M. (2010). *1 & 2 Timothy Titus.* Scottsdale, PA: Herald Press.

# 7

# Biblical Servant Leadership

What is biblical servant leadership? Is it servant leadership that has been discussed in the models with their connections to each other but as critiqued and expanded by the teachings of Scripture? In this search through biblical servant leadership the texts describe many aspects of leadership and aspects of servant leadership as well. The concepts are diverse and look at diverse levels of leadership: from leadership preparation to leadership legacy, from behaviors to internal issues like motives and even attitudes. These biblical constructs and designs fit well with the overall concept of servant leadership as well as with some of the individual issues of servant leadership. In this process is found a finely nuanced way of leadership that is biblical servant leadership.

## Biblical Concepts for Servant Leadership

In these biblical concepts are found not only virtues and constructs but methods of learning leadership. Jesus used the method of modeling which would include several current ideas like mentoring and action learning, but it expands these with concepts about the effectiveness of the "follow me" method. Both Old and New Testaments endorse servant leadership

© The Author(s) 2018
S. Crowther, *Biblical Servant Leadership*, Christian Faith Perspectives in
Leadership and Business, https://doi.org/10.1007/978-3-319-89569-7_7

and give insights into both the model and the process of servant leadership. It is apparent from these studies that love is paramount in servant leadership along with the other virtues of servant leadership like humility, altruism, trust, empowering others, and service to others. The core issue for many of these texts is upon the focus on the followers in caring for them, empowering them, and protecting them. The Scriptures heartily endorse servant leadership, however, with some nuances and expansions.

There are many internal issues that become important in this biblical concept of servant leadership that are not directly addressed in the servant leadership models. The internal issues of integrity and forgiveness come to the forefront here as of prime importance. These were the issues that kept Joseph's leadership on track for long term, even building a leadership legacy. There are other internal issues of character development as well, including perseverance as a key to character development and overcoming opposition. Included in these internal issues would be the issue of being blameless or not easily accused of wrongdoing. Nevertheless, the list goes on, including overcoming the motive of greed and self-focus and it even enters the area of proper attitude. This focuses on the need that is seen in many of these leaders' lives for proper preparation for leadership. Even the ideal leader of the suffering servant in Isaiah is the ultimate servant leader; yet, suffering is part of this process for him. It is more than learning right behaviors and responses; it is developing a foundation for this servant leadership built on virtues and results in serving others. Leadership is seen as ontological in nature in that it proceeds from the being of the leader not just the doing or the saying of the leader. How is this accomplished? The Scripture helps at this juncture as well through story and direct teaching. In learning to deal properly with hardship and suffering, the leader develops perseverance, which produces character, hope and even love is shed through the person in this process. It is not that leaders need to seek suffering; there is plenty out here already. However, the leader must learn to persevere instead of become a victim through bitterness. This is part of the learning process for servant leaders to prepare them to lead from the heart. There is a further issue of learning as the leader is transformed by renewing of the mind. This involves information, but it also involves growth through knowing and experiencing more of the knowledge of the Lord, knowledge of life, and even knowledge of how to lead. The mind is part of the soul that needs transformation as well; it needs change, and it cannot just be left to circumstantial experience. This is the first nuance.

When the issue of love comes up, everyone has their own definition. The Scripture must be able to define love as it is used in the text. It is not just any definition that comes from the latest movie or book. The key to love is developing godly character. Love without character is a beginning but love can only fully express itself through good character since love is the ultimate in other orientation. However, love has no follow-through power without good character and the ability to overcome self-focus. This is found in the Scripture as well in that the enemy of servant leadership is self-focus and self-exaltation. In servant leadership, one is looking for that natural desire to serve, according to Greenleaf (2002). However, what if that natural desire is not there? Does that mean that servant leadership is only limited to those with this natural desire? No, of course not, but it asks the question of whether this heart concept can be developed. According to this study, it can be developed; in fact, it is assumed that this way of leading will be developed by the leaders in Scripture. The power of servant leadership is found in love but character must be developed to support this power of love. This concept of love from the Scripture must be addressed from Scripture for a proper understanding of this foundational concept for effective leadership. This issue will be addressed later in this study.

Moses was a good example of a servant leaders and his humility resulted in not only an ability to work with others but also the ability to empower others through delegation and developing other leaders. He gave power away to thousands of other leaders. Part of his leadership journey was that he was living out a call from God and he was helping others lead and find their calling as well. Leaders develop a sense of purpose through their own calling and help others by empowering them not only by giving power away but also by helping each find their purpose in their leadership. This is seen not only in the life of Moses but also in Esther, Peter, Paul, and other biblical leaders. Calling is a biblical concept but everyone has a sense of calling or a desire for purpose and this sense of something bigger is in all human hearts. This issue of calling was important in biblical leaders but it is important for leaders today as well. Servant leaders find their call in leading and help others find their call as well. This is part of the focus on and care for others.

Particularly in the Old Testament, God is seen as the ultimate leader. His leadership brings the picture of the shepherd leader to the discussion in that He was the ultimate shepherd leader but he called His leaders to be shepherd leaders as well. Is shepherd leadership different than servant leadership? They both share a focus on others. In shepherd leadership, the leader is called the servant of the Lord but in serving the Lord the shepherd serves people. These shepherd leaders are called upon to feed the sheep, to care for them, to heal them, and to gather them. In other words, much like servant leaders, shepherd leaders are called to focus on followers and to overcome self-focus. However, there is a further development for shepherd leaders in the instruction to guide the people as well. This guide would include giving instructions and direction. This would be more of a focus on the future for the followers as to direction for them and for the nation or for the mission of the organization. Is there guidance in servant leadership? It could be implied but it is not explicit. It is possible that biblical servant leadership would include more direction from the leader for the individual and for the group.

One of the issues of servant leadership found is that of a search for wisdom in being able to discern right from wrong in serving the people. This is wisdom with practical applications and today it would be called ethics. However, it is not just business ethics with its cultural contingencies; it is biblical ethics in the ability to know the difference between right and wrong and to use that wisdom in a proper way. This is the issue that got the human race in trouble in the beginning when Adam and Eve bit the forbidden fruit believing they would be like God, knowing good and evil (Genesis 3:5). That ability to know the difference has been distorted since that moment and humans are still working it out. So, to do this well, the leader needs good ethical biblical wisdom in the ability to know right from wrong. Some would think that this goes without needing to be mentioned but this is not true. Ethics can no longer be an adjunct to leadership; it must become part of the models and it can begin with biblical servant leadership.

In leadership and in leadership development, the Lord shows concern for leadership legacy and developing successors in leadership. This was the failure of Gideon and part of the success of Moses. Moses' successor, Joshua, carried on in leading Israel for another 40 years after the death of Moses. This developed stability in the people as individuals and in the nation of Israel. Servant leaders tend to develop other servant leaders and even develop servant leadership in whole organizations. Nevertheless, there needs to be a future focus as well on developing successor leaders. Included in this is that servant leadership needs to be intentional in developing servant leaders, helping others find the path to effective leadership through serving as is found in the Levites of Israel and as was failed by Elisha's servant.

Jesus becomes the ultimate servant leader and he endorses becoming great through becoming a servant. With Jesus it is more than serving—it is becoming a servant, it is ontological, it involves who one becomes as a person. Then leadership proceeds from the person of the leader. He even models servant leadership in foot washing and calls his disciples to deeper levels of leading by giving up their lives in the leading and shepherding, caring for others. Jesus chooses a path of no reputation rather than grasping what is His and His obedience is even to death. He calls his disciples to become this kind of leader in following his example. Even Paul later tells the leaders to have this same attitude as Christ. It is attitude, but it is also in giving up prestige and honor for the sake of serving others. This is a profound serving position. This model becomes deeply personal based upon internal issues of motive and desire. The constant exhortation to leaders is for them to overcome greed, self-focus, and self-exaltation. This way of servant leading is the heart of that call. The instruction to shepherd and serve was given to leaders and they mostly failed however; Jesus came and not only taught but lived the model of servant leadership. This model though involves the transformation of the very deep recesses of the human soul. However, can this be done in the present context of contemporary life and leadership? Yes, it can. This nuance is that servant leadership must become ontological to be able to be the profound servant leadership in the biblical model of Jesus.

When Jesus sends his followers to lead and disciple others, he does it based on his authority. Here, in Jesus is seen the proper use of and submission to authority. In several places in both Old and New Testaments, the leaders are told not to domineer in the use of authority. Proper use of authority is an issue for biblical leadership however; it does not appear in servant leadership. The proper use of authority for guidance and encouragement instead of for dominance and fear needs to be addressed in the model of leadership. Power is always an issue in leadership and teaching even servants how to use it well can be important. Stewards as found in 1 Peter 4 were lead servants. They had to learn to use authority properly since it was delegated authority. However, the only one with pure undelegated power is the Lord and all other power is delegated. Some of the issues of power are implied and discussed in servant leadership nevertheless; a biblical nuance would be to add a segment with insights for the proper use of authority.

Along with proper use of authority is the issue of gifts given to each person. In Scripture, these are called spiritual gifts and they come from God but everyone has differing gifts even natural gifts. These gifts help the leader do well and even excel at leading. The key here is for the leaders to find the gifts given to them and use them well; even finding ways for them to grow while helping others find their gifts. The key is to do this with humility and not self-proclamation. The servant leader serves others by helping them find and develop both calling and gifting.

Finally, Paul instructs leaders to have the goal of bringing maturity in the followers so they can serve others as well. The goal is multiplication. He then gives Timothy strict instructions on developing leaders. These leaders must be blameless with self-control and integrity. The leader must use authority with care and must be mature with humility with a good reputation. These all fit within the purview of servant leadership as nuanced by Scripture. However, Paul goes on to teach that this leader must be able to overcome strategies of the enemy and develop proper strategies. Does this fit or is it a question for another chapter? This is a question that moves beyond expansion and critique of servant leadership to another chapter. This research yields concepts from Scripture for a nuanced model for biblical servant leadership.

# Biblical Love in Leadership

Before moving on to discuss this model of leadership, the issue of biblical love in leadership needs to be developed. New ideas for leadership have been emerging in the twenty-first century. Some of these ideas include concepts of humility, spirituality, and even love. Each of these are important concepts for effective leadership and each needs to be developed from a biblical perspective for biblical leadership. Nevertheless, the issue for the moment is that of love in leadership. This is clearly seen as an issue for leaders in a biblical context. However, the question remains as to what this kind of biblical love looks like and how it interacts with leadership issues and development.

Scripture describes and demonstrates the concept of love in many different ways and contexts. Sometimes the love of God is contrasted with human love as in Romans 5:6–8, where human love could barely give of self for a good person or cause, while divine love gives in Christ giving of self for sinners. God's love is so much greater than human love that it can only be contrasted not compared to human love. This love is powerful in God sending His Son. This love is seen in the life and ministry of Jesus as well. He saw the people as sheep without a shepherd. He saw those that needed help and healing and was moved with compassion like in the case of the widow of Nain in Luke 7 where He had compassion on her and raised her son from the dead. This is the demonstration of love but how can love be described, what are its biblical attributes?

Paul addresses this issue in the ultimate section of love in Scripture in 1 Corinthians 13. This chapter is written in the context of Paul explaining and endorsing spiritual gifts in the previous chapter including supernatural gifts such as healing and leadership gifts such as apostles, prophets, and teachers. Paul here is not calling the love the supreme gift, but rather the way of life for Christ's agent, it is the norm and the guide for the exercise of all gifts (Witherington, 1995). This is the standard for the life and ministry of all believers and it is the standard for those who lead as well.

There are four sections here in this chapter that focuses on love. The first section speaks of the futility of different gifts without love in their application. The second section describes love in both negative and positive concepts. The third section contrasts love with different gifts and the final section displays the greatness of love. It is as if Paul is stretching his rhetorical skills in multiple ways to give a full understanding of this concept of love since it is so central to life. He uses the tools of rhetorical arguments, of contrast as well as comparison and even the tools of poetic description in describing love. This is such an important concept and yet one that is so easily misunderstood and manipulated for self-gain that it needs a full-orbed explanation. Commentators have long noticed the more elevated and almost poetic style of this chapter, it is a rhetorical and deliberative piece in exalting love and it is about love as the modus operandi of all gifts (Witherington, 1995). Therefore, this pericope becomes an important component in understanding love in leadership. What's love got to do with it? It has everything to do with servant and biblical leadership in that it is the root and foundation to these models of leadership.

In this section, there are several rhetorical devices that are thickly textured. A few of them will be examined here in this study. There are several issues of Socio-Rhetorical Interpretation in the area of inner texture in this pericope. There is repetitive texture with a focus on the word "love." There is an open-middle-closing texture that begins with showing love as a necessary foundation for the gifts then moving through the middle of describing love in several ways then in the closing of the praise of love as the preeminent issue of life and the use of the gifts including the gifts of leadership. This brings the question to the front as to how leadership is a gift or involves gifts. However, for the moment the focus is on this foundation of love for leadership. In addition, there is a progressive texture moving from seeing love as necessary to the understanding of love finally to the revelation that love is the greatest attribute in life and by implication in leadership.

There are three statements about the gifts without love. Then there are seven positive statements about love and eight negative statements showing the contrast of love in the opposite of love. Each of these attributes is also seen in other texts of Scripture either by example or explanation (Fisk, 2000). Love is then compared to three gifts of prophesy, tongues, and the gift of knowledge. Finally, love is compared to the two important issues of faith and hope while being declared greater than these other two important issues.

In the midst of these rhetorical devices, it is found that this chapter on love is a central issue in 1 Corinthians overall since it is the center of a chiastic structure. This chiastic structure begins in Chap. 11 and ends in Chap. 14 with Chap. 13 being the focal point in the center of the structure as a hymn to love (Bailey, 2011). In the midst of this chiastic structure, the section on love has a further chiastic structure. It is a chiasm in a chiasm. A chiastic structure is a rhetorical device with a certain form that focuses on the middle of the information in the structure but it is recognized and developed by a certain form or style. For instance, in 1 Corinthians 13 section a is in 13:1–3 on love and spiritual gifts, b is love defined positively in 13:4a, c is love defined negatively in 13:4b–13:6, b' is love defined positively and a' is love and spiritual gifts (Bailey, 2011). The two "a" sections are about similar issues and the two "b" sections are about similar issues and the "c" section stands alone. The focus is on the middle. The focus here is the description or even the definition of love. Love is primary for Paul because it has already been given concrete expression in the coming of Jesus Christ to die for the sins of the world, love is more than an idea because love is an act and this is the way the gifts are to function and this is how love functions in building the community (Fee, 2014). Love as found in 1 Corinthians is a heart issue but it is an issue that finds its way to action in building others and in building the group or the community.

First in interpretation it is important to notice the word here used for love. Paul uses the verb *agapao* here, but the contemporary Greek language used two other words for love: one was for passionate love and the other for the description of friendship (Bailey, 2011). This clear definition of godly love needed a new platform. This new word was a rare word from classical Greek having to do with "inclining toward," but Paul and other writers of Scripture filled it with meaning (Bailey, 2011). 1 Corinthians 13 is one of those places that fills this word with new meaning. The first three verses describe gifts being used without love and this then is an empty even a useless endeavor. Then the text moves on rapidly to give definition to this special word for love.

The positive descriptions of definition for love open and close this section with the negatives in the middle and the center is split with the single line: "not seeking what is for itself" which reflects the issue of the homily

(Bailey, 2011). This pericope has a series of 15 verbs in describing love and this passage easily transcends the immediate situation giving it universal appeal (Fee, 2014). Remember this Greek word used here is a verb and 15 verbs are used to describe and define it. This is significant in that this issue of the heart is turned into action in this kind of love. The first two qualities are patience and kindness. This represents love's active and passive responses toward others, the first is to forbear with others and the second is to extend mercy through kindness (Fee, 2014). The text then turns to issues that are not actions of love. It is possible that these are expressions of how to be patient and kind with others. Notice the first section is that love is something then the next section describes what love does not do to others. It could be read that love is kind and patient and the way this love is expressed is by not being jealous, boastful, arrogant (or proud), rude, self-seeking, easily provoked (or angered) or the one who keeps track of wrongs. Love can absorb evil, love manages to erase the ledger of wrongs suffered (Bailey, 2011). Then finally, this love does not rejoice in unrighteousness or evil but then the list turns positive again.

In the positive list, this list begins with love rejoicing with truth. Notice the contrast here is between evil and truth, not evil and goodness. So, how is truth the opposite of evil? Here Paul is reflecting the character of God which is to be displayed by His people and such a person refuses to take delight in evil and takes delight in victories, in mercy and justice even for those with whom one disagrees (Fee, 2014). This rejoicing in truth will help the person bear or cover all things. One way to translate this section is that love covers all things or protects all and because you cover others then you are trustworthy (Bailey, 2011). People need others they can trust to cover them and bear with them in all different circumstances, this is love. Then love believes all things hopes all things and ultimately endures all things. This is the character of love to "put up" with everything, love has a tenacity in the present, buoyed by its absolute confidence in the future that enables it to pour itself out in behalf of others and in essence love never loses hope (Fee, 2014). Love is a powerful force that can overcome evil and even suffering and it has some basic attributes of godly character. Love moves past a heart issue to a heart issue that has powerful actions in both positive ways toward others and in negative ways in issues that are avoided.

Then love is contrasted with different gifts and shown to be more effective and resilient even than gifts that are divinely given to individuals. Gifts and talents are not the best part of the person. Love that results in real actions and in real self-control is the best part of the person and of the leader as well. Then finally, love is considered with two other eternal and foundational issues in that of faith and hope. All three are eternal issues. However, faith will become sight in eternity and hope will become fulfilled but love remains. The greatest is love. This is not just greatness for the future, but it is greatness for the present. Having affirmed that love is the highest of all, Paul urges his readers to "run after love" in 1 Corinthians 14:1 (Bailey, 2011).

Love that is biblical is filled with meaning and very specific issues of action and attitude. These issues cannot be arbitrarily changed by culture or society. Society and leaders can learn from this description of divine love or *agapao* to be able to love well even in the midst of cultural ambiguity and change. Love is a powerful force that is patient and kind. This love is not self-seeking and yet manifests in overcoming these human tendencies toward pride, jealousy, rudeness, and keeping track of wrongs. Love absorbs evil and has a capacity to put up with things and people that are difficult and this love is able to pour itself out for the sake of others following the example of Jesus Christ who came and demonstrated true, deep, real love. This is the foundation for biblical servant leadership. Run after love.

# The Difference and the Cohesion in the Servant Leadership Models

There are several concepts that need attention in their connections between servant leadership and the teachings of Scripture. These are issues like humility, love, self-issues, confidence as well as issues of ontology and how to teach servant leadership. Granted there are differences in some of the models of servant leadership; however, in examining the Scriptures there are ways to bring cohesion from a divine perspective on leadership. The way forward is to continue to critique these models in light of the overarching teaching of Scriptures on this issue. In this place is found that servant leadership is a virtuous theory with several aspects of leadership that proceed from this foundation.

# Moving from Concept to Application

However, the biblical concept goes deeper to issues of character and formation. The concept of godly character becomes the root from which the virtues and other centeredness spring. In overcoming conflicts and differences, there is also the issue of definitions. He who writes the definitions wins the argument. For instance, love is defined in so many diverse ways and applied in some bizarre ways. Therefore, the definitions must have divine roots as found in Scripture and this must be done carefully to overcome existing biases in the researcher. How can this model be applied? It must be applied ontologically. In other words, ways must be found in leadership development in this model that the person is changed in the area of the soul. Part of this change comes from spiritual formation and addressing the issues of the soul. This is very personal and individual but it can be done. Character can even be developed as leaders learn to deal well with difficulties and learn the secret of perseverance. However, the issue is whether the model as found in Scripture is servant leadership or some other more biblical model of leadership. In Scripture, there is found a more robust model that includes issues of serving but moves beyond servant leadership as found in the contemporary models.

The biblical model for servant leadership is a very detailed model; however, it can clearly be shown in stages. The preparation stage or the pre-leadership stage involves developing the internal issues of character, forgiveness, and integrity along with the other internal issues that relate to this deep soul development through an understanding of suffering and developing a proper worldview. Then the foundation is further developed by love, matured by character that fits within the parameters of biblical love. Then these work together in developing an ontological change from transformation of the soul in becoming a servant, which is more than serving. The how of this development can vary with the experience or trajectory of the person but it is a transformative world that involves renewing of the mind and soul that brings internal real second order change. First, order change just changes externals like moving the furniture around in a room. Second, order change is deep real change like rebuilding the room in the house.

The second stage is the leadership stage itself where the person is a leader on some level. In addition, this would be where these attributes form the internal work would grow and mature in the leader. There is one aspect that bridges the gap between the first and second stage in that of calling. The calling of a leader begins in the preparation stage as part of this process in stage 1. However, this calling spans into the second stage as the person begins to lead based in calling and purpose. Calling helps to set the trajectory for where the leader is going to lead as well as sets the stage for the other virtues and attributes in leading. Knowing personal calling helps the leader lead with security and in helping others find calling as well. This becomes part of the vision aspect in servant leadership in vision and development for the followers. Then as in the virtue theory of servant leadership, love is the first virtue or the foundational virtue. From this virtue flows two streams into more virtues and also several attributes that then fully develop service. In the virtue stream are humility and altruism which develop vision for the follower and trust giving way for empowerment to others and ultimately service. Then in the attributes stream from love flows proper use of authority and guidance, proper use of gifts, and proper use of ethics or wisdom. These attributes then lead to empowerment of others and service. Together these streams of virtues and attributes come together in empowerment and service of others.

There is a final or a third stage. This stage begins during the second stage but becomes well developed toward the end of the second stage. This is the development of a legacy of leadership. The leader trains and equips other leaders as part of the organizational and servant leadership process during the entire second stage. This is part of the proper use of authority, guidance, and gifts. Nevertheless, the leader must develop other leaders who can replace or improve upon her/his present leadership. Success is having a successor as seen in Moses and Joshua, so it is with all leaders. This stage can take many forms but it only comes to full fruition once the leader has moved on to other areas of life or leadership. These three stages come together to form a robust model for biblical servant leadership which can be seen in Fig. 7.1.

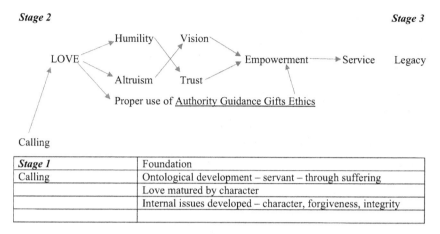

**Fig. 7.1** Biblical servant leadership

# Application in the Business World

This concept of leadership can then be applied in the business world like the original model was applied at AT&T. As Christians learn to be servant leaders and lead in this way in the context of the world of business with results it will bring attention to this way of leading. Biblical servant leadership is a construct of leadership that concerns the internal motive issues of leadership. This type of leadership can be used in diverse organizational contexts whether church, business, education, or government. The core components are internal yet manifest in certain leadership functions. These leadership functions can be done as a result of a leader's job description but this misses the point of biblical servant leadership. Biblical servant leadership is driven by purpose as revealed and delegated through individuals. This type of leadership comes from calling, an ongoing encounter, and a life of love as developed with good character and a life of humility. The development for this type of leadership involves transformation through mind renewal and a new way of dealing with suffering of past, present, and future issues. Can these attributes be gained by those who are not Christians? These functions can be developed by all and God has destiny over people who are not believers. In addition, they can develop certain important internal qualities as well. This model can be used in the business world and other areas of leadership that are not in the church. It can be used among believers and those who are not followers of Christ. However, the context of the church and Christian ministry provides a rich context for the development and application of this model of leadership where it can be lived out in real contexts of leadership.

## Application in the Church World

Then in the church this needs to become an issue of leadership. Perhaps this model can provide a way of leading that overcomes the dark side of leadership which causes many leaders to fail. The dark side of leadership is when leaders become successful but are not prepared for success. The result is that this success pulls on the darker side of the human nature and this can even happen in servant leadership if the leader is not properly prepared for this rush of success. The leadership world has equipped and trained people and even organizations for success. However, this training normally does not include preparation in the soul of the leader for this desired result. Many are good at teaching leaders to succeed but not so good at preparing leaders how to handle success when it comes. This darker side of leadership is called toxic or narcissistic leadership and it happens often which then short circuits leaders and organizations. This concept of biblical servant leadership prepares the individual to succeed as a leader and prepares the person for that success when it comes. This occurs through developing humility and overcoming dangerous self-focus issues with a development of character that brings effective perseverance in times of suffering and celebration. This is a custom model for the church where leadership development can include character development and other internal issues of development. It is a good way ahead for the church in leadership that imitates biblical models of leadership that are counterintuitive and countercultural but have been effective for over 4000 years. Four thousand years of effective leadership with all of its negatives and pitfalls shown in the human experience is quite an important heritage. In this way, the church could lead in leadership and not be simply the distant follower of culture and follow Jesus' command not to lead as the world leads but lead as servant of all, like He did.

# Conclusion

This study of many texts of Scripture reveals a certain divine perspective concerning leadership. This divine perspective unfolds over the centuries and becomes more explicit in the New Testament. Nevertheless, from the beginning, Scripture has discussed leadership in many contexts beginning with Adam and Eve and continuing with Jesus and the apostles through the Book of Revelation. This discussion of leadership has taken on many forms from examples to mandates to instructions even with rebukes at times for leaders who are to be biblical leaders. This model of biblical servant leadership is found to be multifaceted, complex, and yet robust and practical. This model can provide a way ahead for more research and for a development process for leadership training in biblical servant leadership that addresses internal issues, values and even important biblical leadership attributes with an eye on the future for the development of generational success in leadership.

There is more research needed in that there are many more examples and texts in Scripture that need to be examined then compared and contrasted with current research. This research needs to include theological depth as well as an understanding of twenty-first-century cultural and leadership issues. There is still a journey ahead in this process in testing and developing this model for leadership and leadership development. Journeys like this are always filled with surprises, epiphanies, and pitfalls. However, it is the joy of the journey, discovery, and even of growth that adds great value to this journey. This intersection between Scripture and leadership is just such a journey, a joyful, fruitful journey with wonderful surprises and detours along the way. There is even more good news though, in that the journey itself is formational. The process changes us. We are those who dream of a better future. Let us see the vision of a better future for leadership and biblical leadership and then let us create this new future in our generation.

# References

Bailey, K. E. (2011). *Paul Through Mediterranean Eyes: Cultural Studies in 1 Corinthians*. Downers Grove, IL: InterVarsity Press.

Fee, G. D. (2014). *The First Epistle to the Corinthians, Revised Edition (The New International Commentary on the New Testament)*. Grand Rapids, MI: Wm. B. Eerdman's Press.

Fisk, B. N. (2000). *First Corinthians (Interpretation Bible Studies)*. Louisville, KY: Geneva Press.

Greenleaf, R. (2002). *Servant Leadership: A Journey into the Nature of Legitimate Power and Greatness*. Mahwah, NJ: Paulist Press.

Witherington, B. (1995). *Conflict and Community in Corinth: A Socio-Rhetorical Commentary on 1 and 2 Corinthians*. Grand Rapids, MI: Wm. B. Eerdman's Press.

# 8

# A Call for Biblical Leadership

## Existing Research on Biblical Leadership

In the context of leadership studies, there have been several examinations of biblical leadership from the analysis of different texts of Scripture. These studies have revealed a rich fabric of leadership principles for the present issue of a biblical model of leadership. Some of these studies have developed separate models of leadership, while others have found principles for leadership and even leadership development. These studies include exegetical studies like the study from Bekker (2006), while others are longitudinal qualitative studies that include an analysis of leaders in the biblical text like the work from Clinton (2012). In addition, there are dissertations on leadership as taught by Jesus, Paul, or Peter as well as works on leadership characteristics from Old Testament figures like King David (Serrano, 2017).

© The Author(s) 2018
S. Crowther, *Biblical Servant Leadership*, Christian Faith Perspectives in Leadership and Business, https://doi.org/10.1007/978-3-319-89569-7_8

# Moving on in Biblical Leadership

There is a great amount of insight to be gained from these existing studies. Nevertheless, there is more to be gained from viewing these studies together for insights from convergence and distinction in these examinations of Scripture. Then, as was found in this study, there is more that can be gleaned from a close examination of the text to include issues of shepherding and character. How could these principles be used in a contemporary context? Are there any organizations that are using this way or concept of leading? These are important questions of application. There are several leadership principles here that can be located in a beginning model. This model would include issues like humility, the proper use of power, developing perseverance through suffering, developing character in life situations, steward leadership as well as servant leadership concepts.

In addition to these servant leadership components, there were also found in this study other important components of leadership that would expand into a biblical model of leadership that would include and interact with the biblical servant model of leadership or the other components found in the previous chapter. First among these components is the issue of vision. In servant leadership, the vision is for the followers but then there is a secondary goal for the organization and the community. However, in biblical leadership, as the study moves into the life of Jesus and the teachings of the New Testament, vision for the mission becomes very much a component of leadership in the life of Jesus and of Paul. This answers the question of vision in the servant leadership literature concerning organizational vision. The vision here in Scripture is vision for the mission that drives the organization. Jesus' vision was to make disciples in all ethnic groups on the earth. He repeated this in several ways and in different contexts. This was not a lone vision but a shared vision as well with billions of followers through the ages with this same vision. The result is the building of the church throughout the centuries. The result of His vision is the church is built against all odds. This is leadership. This is similar to the concept to inspirational motivation of transformational leadership.

The second component is that biblical leaders are encouraged to become models for others to follow in Hebrews 13:7. Then Paul and Jesus both use the mode of follow me in mentoring others for ministry resulting in legacy as mentioned in the last section. Peter even exhorts believers and leaders to "follow in His (exact) steps" (1 Peter 2:21). Nevertheless, it is also the way of leading in the present tense for biblical leaders as well. This modeling worked well for Jesus and Paul in multiplying leaders for the rapidly growing ministry and church. This is similar to idealized influence in transformational leadership.

In the third component is found a concept of developing strategy. This is found in Paul describing the qualifications of leaders when he includes a strategic portion in his description to Timothy. These qualified leaders must maintain a good reputation for those outside the church and to actively overcome the strategies set against them and develop proper strategies for the advance of the church. There is a strategic component here in two ways. One is overcoming problems and two is developing ways into the future for the expansion of the organization. Jesus in his leadership was helping the disciples and the nation to see old problems in a new way. He solved many puzzles and dilemmas for the disciples like how it was hard for the rich to get into the Kingdom. This was not a statement against wealthy people though it may be read this way through twenty-first-century cultural lenses. The problem for the disciples was they wrongly believed if one was rich, that person was blessed by God because they were closer to God. Conversely, if they were poor, they were far from God as evidenced by the lack of blessing. This is why they were astonished and responded to Jesus by saying, "Who can be saved" (Mark 10:26)? Yet Jesus was also challenging, pushing them to new ideas like the need for new wine skins in Mark 2:22 to receive the new wine of the gospel. The old wine skins were some of their old religious ways and these had to change to move forward with the Lord. Jesus was a problem solver and an innovator. This is similar intellectual stimulation in transformational leadership.

The fourth element of transformational leadership is individualized consideration, but this is clearly present in all of the discussions in Scripture concerning servant and shepherd leadership. However, there is a fourth component clearly present in both Old and New Testaments that ground biblical leadership in spirituality. Spiritual formation is important and found in the practical aspect in the development of the internal issues of the person as found in the previous section. There is more though. Moses, Gideon, even Samson, Jesus, and Paul all had these personal encounters with the Lord that were very pivotal and real. This type of connection to the Lord continued through their lives and it manifest in issues like being able to change even in difficult situations but more than that it manifest in faith. It manifest in an attitude of confidence in God, an adjusted attitude of self-efficacy. In the purpose of God this can be accomplished was the attitude of each of these leaders and others as well. This gave these leaders the proper balance between confidence and humility. This is a difficult characteristic to develop in that it can become either arrogance or negligence. Arrogance in being overcome with pride and negligence in becoming inactive waiting for something to happen. The balance is confident humility.

This develops a robust model for biblical leadership. This model follows the biblical servant leadership model with three stages but with these additions mentioned above and some other aspects of Christian spirituality in both the foundation and the process of leadership in stages 1 and 2. The first two aspects of spirituality would be established in the foundation or stage 1. This is a robust faith and connection to and encounter with the Lord. This is found in leaders from Old to New Testaments and is of primary importance. Without faith and trust in God that others can imitate biblical leadership loses its vitality. This faith in the Lord Jesus Christ manifests in many externals but it is an internal foundational issue first and helps to develop the other important foundational internal issues. The second foundational issue found in many biblical leaders is that they were each servants to the Lord first before they were servants to the people. The biblical leader must develop an attitude like that of Jesus Christ Himself of being a servant to God first. In addition, in the foundational phase, there is the issue of learning to manage the family well, in learning to lead with authority in a proper way. The final addition is found in the process of leadership as found in stage 2. In biblical leadership, the goal or the end or the teleology of leadership is not just for service to others nor to meet the goals of the mission. The ultimate goal of biblical leadership is to bring glory to God. This means to not only bring honor to God in all that is done and even to look for ways to honor God, but it also means to bring clarity to who God is and how He interacts with people. The biblical leader is to lead with the glory of God as the motive and goal in all of the processes of being and doing. The word "glory" describes the superlative honor that should be given to God by everything in the universe and it can also be the created brightness that surrounds God's revelation of Himself (Grudem, 1994). These are two definitions of the glory of God but can be seen together in that giving honor to God helps humans see this revelation of God. This then is the motive to bring honor to God and in the process help people grasp more fully the revelation of God. This glory of God is the manifestation of the excellence of God's character and greatness of being which we cannot fully comprehend, but we can stand in awe and worship (Grudem, 1994). Love in leadership then is not only the motive it is the goal in showing others about God's real love and care for people. This biblical model for leadership can be seen in Fig. 8.1.

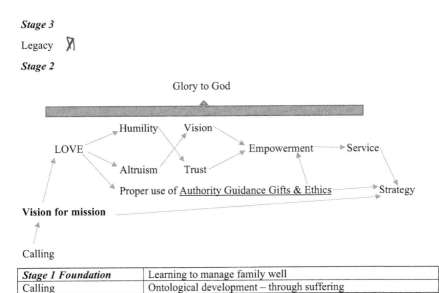

Fig. 8.1  Biblical leadership

In this model, the process of leadership develops in the overall areas of glory to God, service to others, and strategic futures for the mission. This model could then be used for leadership development in these specific areas of life and leading.

## Application of Biblical Leadership

This way of leading could be developed over time using mentoring concepts. Concerning leadership outcomes, many declare mentoring a proven method for developing people for leadership (Goleman, Boyatzis, & Mckee, 2002; Malpurs, 1999; Noe, 1999). Mentoring has positive effects for leadership development for individuals including ministers. O'Daniel (2005) found that a great majority (89%) of the ministers surveyed in the UPCI (United Pentecostal Church International) said they would not be in leadership and ministry if it had not been for their mentors. Mentoring is an important method for training as found in the Scriptures. A survey of biblical figures and Christian leaders underscores the conclusion that one of the major influences in developing a leader is a person or persons who have something to share that the leader needs, a mentor (Stanley & Clinton, 1992). Some biblical examples of this are Moses mentoring Joshua, Barnabas mentoring Paul, and then Paul mentoring Timothy. Mentors were important for leadership development in the church in its early form. Mentors are also important for the development of ministers for leadership in the modern context. Mentoring research has shown mentoring to be influential in developing leaders, and research in a large energy company found that leaders with significant levels of leadership strengths attributed their development to mentoring early in their careers (O'Daniel, 2005). According to Stanley and Clinton (1992), one of the important factors of leaders who finished well and continued in the learning and growth process was that of having several important mentors during their lifetime.

Many of these concepts for leadership have been used in Manna Church. This church has developed its own leadership pipeline with these issues of leadership in the heart of the training. This is one of the 100 largest and fastest-growing churches in the United States and was founded

in the 1970s but has not undergone leadership change due to failure of the leader. Many of the leaders are trained within the context of the organization. Then the organization works with a college in further developing these potential leaders in the areas of theology, life, and leadership. The application of biblical leadership can be done in this contemporary context though it will need to be done intentionally with careful consideration for proper development and with the understanding that in some ways it will be countercultural. This is a multilevel robust yet complex model for leadership. Nevertheless, it is biblical in nature and is a long process of preparation and it is living in leadership. The person becomes a leader with complex issues at work both internally and externally addressing the issues of Christian spirituality, self, motive, and the proper use of divergent areas such as authority and ethics. This complexity makes it difficult to conceptualize but not impossible. This complexity makes it even harder to do this way of leading but not impossible. With the proper vision for biblical leadership, it can not only be accomplished but it can grow and prosper in different areas beginning in the church and different ministries. It can also be taken into the business world as Christian leaders adopt this for themselves and then become leaders in many diverse business, education, and government organizations. In this way, we can see leadership from the divine perspective. In this way, we can develop Christian leadership to be able to lead in the leadership world. The way into the future for this way of leadership is for leaders in the church to begin to live this model then to set forth the example for the next generation of leaders in colleges and churches as well as in businesses. This is a process and not an immediate solution and it is costly on a personal level, but it is the way into the future for the church as the leaders follow Jesus' example of leading the church and teaching others to lead.

## Biblical Leadership: Pioneers or Settlers

In the search for a biblical model of leadership, the material for research is vast and this study is not the conclusion of the matter; it is simply part of a very long journey of discovery and adaptation to the new concepts. In this search, there are issues that come to the surface that are not addressed in leadership or ethical theories yet and need some discussion and study. One of these areas is found in the diversity of leaders in both the Old and New Testaments. This is not about the diversity of their cultural heritage or their connection to the tribal system of Israel. It is more about the kind or type of leaders and how they lead. It is about leadership but it is not about a model of leadership or the culture that is set by leadership or even the climate of a group in response to a leader or leaders. It is related more to the ontology of the leaders and who the leaders are not just in person or style but who they are in motivation and how they lead. This can be seen in Scripture in the different leaders and how they lead. Paul begins to explain this concept in 1 Corinthians. In chapter 3, Paul is discussing his ministry and the ministry of Apollos in connection to the Corinthians. In verse 5, he calls both of them servants through whom they believed. Paul and Apollos were both servants of the Lord and servant leaders to the Corinthians. Yet there was a difference. This difference actually was causing a division in the church. The people in the church were forming factions or siding with certain leaders against each other. Neither Paul nor Apollos were developing or endorsing this division but it was happening around them and their different leadership styles. This was not a difference in leadership models like a difference between transformational and servant leadership. Paul would have solved this issue differently. Instead, this was an issue in how they led differently and Paul addresses this issue directly.

Paul tells the Corinthians in chapter 3 verse 6 that he had planted and Apollos watered but it was God who gave the increase. Paul and Apollos had different aspects of leadership in the church but both were needed and both had value though this should not bring division. In this section of Scripture in chapter 3 verses 5 through 9, there are several repetitions of inner texture as well as a progressive texture. The repetitions include words like "God," "Paul," and "Apollos," "watered" and "planted." Then the progressive texture begins in verse 5 by asking the question of the identity of Paul and Apollos and ends with giving a definitive answer in verse 9. The progression begins by describing both Paul and Apollos as servants, then in the next section, it tells what they do through the analogy of farming, then it moves in the third section focusing on God as the source and finally in the last section unity is the issue and both types of these leaders are needed to establish God's field (Bailey, 2011). These servant leaders have an important and special but different function with the purpose of building God's field, his church. It is the Lord who makes it work. They are equal and important but different. Does this difference matter? It does matter.

Paul then changes the metaphor to that of a building in verse 9 and he describes the work that he does as the one who lays the foundation of the building and then others (like Apollos) need to come and build upon that foundation. The farm or the building must be built well, and it takes specialists who are experts to build well. It is God working through them but you need a wise master builder to lay the foundation. Paul is the expert at laying the foundation. Apollos is the expert at finishing the building. There are those like Paul that lay a good foundation; these are wise builders that build the proper foundation. This word indicates that this person is both architect and chief engineer and Paul says this is according to the grace or gift given to him, this is a specific grace for this purpose of building the foundation of churches (Fee, 2014). Then there are those like Apollos and others who build on this foundation and the exhortation is to build properly. There are at least two areas seen here of a specific leadership area that transcends models of leadership. Some leaders plant and others water. There is no conflict or competition here between Apollos and Paul though there was between the Corinthian believers. This was the purpose of Paul's exhortation first to correct the Corinthians way of thinking about leaders. Paul and Apollos were not contrary to one another as servant leaders. They worked together in tandem to build the field of the Lord. However, there were others who tried to build on the foundation that Paul laid but unlike Apollos they were building incorrectly. The second reason for this exhortation was to instruct those who would lead in how to build correctly on the foundation.

Rather than foundation layers and builders, a more appropriate description would be pioneers and builders. Are there other examples of these different kinds of leaders in Scripture? This difference can be seen in James, the head of the church at Jerusalem as a builder, and Peter the pioneer, who established churches in many places even crossing cultural lines to do so. Timothy and Titus are sent and instructed by Paul to build where he had pioneered or planted. In addition, there are some who can fill both functions and roles but this is not the norm. Paul did not change to become the builder, he worked with builders. Nehemiah was one who was a pioneer, getting the wall started and completed and he was a builder as well in establishing order and growth in Jerusalem. C. Peter Wagner introduced the concept in his early church growth books about leaders who were pioneers or settlers. The pioneers were the innovators and the growth leaders, whereas the settlers did not do as well in church growth areas. However, this biblical concept moves beyond this concept in seeing both aspects of leadership as effective but different. Is this seen in the contemporary context of leadership? In the church world, there are many small churches that have stopped growing and have hovered between 70 and 150 people in the churches. Some churches are small due to demographics but some possibly need a change from a pioneer leader to a builder leader. This could also be true in businesses and even nonprofits. Perkin and Abraham (2017) discuss a framework for business leaders that includes different types of leaders being pioneers, settlers, or town planners. This is a similar concept based in the business world. Pioneers develop uncharted land, settlers build understanding and make something useful for a larger audience, while town planners find ways to make things faster, better, and more efficient (Perkin & Abraham, 2017). It is possible that these town planners are really builders since builders includes more than the concept of settlers. In this scenario, builders would include both settlers and town planners.

How does this work? The pattern seen in Scripture is that the pioneer goes in and establishes the foundation but he/she also takes several others on that same team. Paul traveled with teams of over 20 people at times during his ministry. In addition, he was consistently leaving or sending leaders to other areas for short or long periods of time. Then he would continue to instruct leaders through writings about how to lead and develop other leaders. Could pioneers become builders and builders become pioneers? This is possible. Possibly, this is what has been seen in the megachurch movement in the United States. Pioneers have learned to become builders as well. It is also possible that these teams at these churches have a good combination of pioneers and builders with each having enough authority to impact the organization. This is an area that needs further research. The business world has seen several rapid successes as well like Amazon or Airbnb. Airbnb is an example in that they own no real estate and they even rent their office space without owning it; yet, they have become a very successful organization. There are many more that could be added to this list like Google, Apple, and Uber. The leaders in these organizations have been able to pioneer and then convert to building rather rapidly. Is this just market forces? There is more here than market forces. It is about leadership.

Understanding this issue of pioneers and builders can bring forward momentum in all types of organizations from churches to schools to businesses. More research is needed both biblically and empirically. However, understanding these issues can bring help in the development of effective leaders for various contexts and callings. In addition, using this concept can help build teams that are very effective in pioneering and building quickly with insights from both the foundational perspective and the building perspective. It can help in the planning stages and of knowing when pioneer leaders are needed and when builder leaders are needed in the organization. Finally, with this understanding developed pioneers could possibly be trained to be builders and builders pioneers. In the early years of leadership theory, it was thought that effective leaders were just born with certain traits and very few could be changed. It would be a mistake to start this process over again concerning pioneers and builders without more research. This leadership concept could change the way business and even church is done and it could bring with it growth, success, and momentum that turns addition growth into multiply growth.

## Conclusion

This is an opportunity for a new model of leadership that includes serving and concepts of servant leadership that is informed, critiqued, and expanded by concepts of biblical leadership. In addition, this concept of pioneers and builders working alongside of this model can create a context for more effective leaders on several levels of leadership bringing multiply-type growth to organizations and churches. Several models of leadership, including servant leadership, have served our organizations and our churches well. Nevertheless, there has been a dark side of leadership that seems difficult to overcome. This soft underside of leadership is found in success. When the leader succeeds, she/he can develop such a self-focus that Narcissistic leadership develops. This form of leading brings destruction to the leader, follower, and the organization. Often the models of leadership do not include development in the internal areas of the person to overcome this narcissistic temptation. This issue in leadership is seen in all types of organizations from government, to business, to the church. The problem is that leadership studies view leadership externally from the results. This is a good beginning but leadership needs to also view the inside of leadership in the person of the leader. Scripture is uniquely qualified in this area since its first concern is the person who leads not just in leadership behaviors. Some models have begun to address this issue recently, but the Scripture gives keen insight into this area of life and leadership. This model of leadership includes several issues that are in the servant leadership model. However, biblical leadership includes other issues as well from the Old Testament shepherd model of leadership that moves beyond the servant mode to the mode of caring direction. It would also include some of the broad issues of New Testament leadership that are transformational and yet include internal issues of character development as well. This is from the principles of leadership as found in both the Old and New Testaments and forms a new model that moves past servant leadership to biblical leadership. This is a model that is ethical, effective, spiritual, and adaptable that helps overcome the human temptation for corruption and self-indulgence.

Both the biblical servant model and the biblical model of leadership can help move leadership studies into the future especially in the area of leadership and its connection to the Scriptures, both Old and New Testaments. This move to a biblical foundation is both important and helpful in seeing leadership from a divine perspective. This is from an outside perspective that takes us out of the human research circle of being both the researcher and the researched. These models though complex and developed in stages can help the research in both biblical studies and leadership research. In addition, they can be developed as models upon which to build leadership development programs and leader education. The way into the future for the human race is effective good leadership.

Our world is filled with divergent troubling issues and many of the solutions need effective, good leaders with a robust way of leading. Looking into the future, which can appear dark at times, is actually very bright. It is an opportunity for new ways of leading with new effective, good leaders to be developed and to rally many of the new effective leaders of the world to bring bright change into our world. In the church, there is a bright future. As the church faces opposition and trouble and even cultural rejection, this is an opportunity for good effective biblical leaders to rise to the surface in the church and ministries to lead in real advance for the Kingdom of God on the earth. These are dark times, these are good times. Frankly, these times inspire me and they should inspire you too.

# References

Bailey, K. E. (2011). *Paul Through Mediterranean Eyes: Cultural Studies in 1 Corinthians*. Downers Grove, IL: InterVarsity Press.

Bekker, C. J. (2006). *The Philippians Hymn (2:5–11) as an Early Mimetic Christological Model of Christian Leadership in Roman Philippi*. Paper presented at the Servant Leadership Research Roundtable.

Clinton, J. R. (2012). *The Making of a Leader*. Colorado Springs, CO: NavPress.

Fee, G. D. (2014). *The First Epistle to the Corinthians, Revised Edition (The New International Commentary on the New Testament)*. Grand Rapids, MI: Wm. B. Eerdman's Press.

Goleman, D., Boyatzis, R. E., & Mckee, A. (2002). *Primal Leadership: Realizing the Power of Emotional Intelligence*. Boston, MA: Harvard Business School Press.

Grudem, W. (1994). *Systematic Theology*. Grand Rapids, MI: Zondervan Publishing House.

Malpurs, A. (1999). *Strategic Planning: A New Model for Church and Ministry Leaders*. Grand Rapids, MI: Baker Books.

Noe, R. A. (1999). *Employee Training and Development*. New York, NY: McGraw-Hill.

O'Daniel, T. R. (2005). *A Relationship Analysis Between Mentoring and Leadership Development Within the United Pentecostal Church International*. Unpublished doctoral dissertation, Southern Baptist Theological Seminary.

Perkin, N., & Abraham, P. (2017). *Building the Agile Business Through Digital Transformation*. New York, NY: Kogan Page.

Serrano, C. (2017). *Leadership Fatigue: What New Leaders Can Learn from an Old King*. Bloomington, IN: WestBow Press.

Stanley, P. D., & Clinton, J. R. (1992). *Connecting: The Mentoring Relationships You Need to Succeed in Life*. Colorado Springs, CO: NavPress.

# Index

## A

*Agapao*, 5, 143, 145
Altruism, 5–7, 14, 26, 33, 52, 136, 147
Argumentative texture, 82, 108,
    110, 113
Authority, 20, 32, 49, 50, 59, 68, 78,
    80, 82, 83, 88, 89, 93, 101,
    106, 121, 122, 140, 147, 156,
    159, 162

## B

Biblical, xiv, xvi, 10, 17, 20, 23, 39,
    53, 54, 70, 72, 88, 89, 97,
    108, 113, 117, 122, 130, 131,
    135–141, 145, 146, 149, 150,
    153–159, 162, 164, 165
Blameless, 117, 123, 136, 140
Business, xiv, xvi, 2, 3, 9, 16–19, 23,
    30, 138, 148–149, 159, 162–164

## C

Call(ing), 2, 6–9, 15, 18, 23, 25, 28,
    33, 39, 40, 44–53, 56, 58, 59,
    63, 65, 66, 70, 71, 81, 91,
    100, 101, 106, 107, 111, 113,
    117, 119, 120, 124, 125, 128,
    129, 137–141, 147–149,
    153–165
Character, xv, 6, 17, 26, 28, 29,
    41–43, 48, 50, 71, 98, 99,
    104–106, 108–110, 112, 113,
    116, 119–123, 128, 130, 136,
    137, 144, 146, 148, 149, 154,
    157, 164
Chiasm, 66, 78, 79, 81, 91,
    115, 143
Christian, xiii–xv, 9, 10, 17, 19–21,
    50, 51, 62, 75, 98, 105, 107,
    111, 113, 116, 124, 148, 149,
    156, 158, 159

© The Author(s) 2018
S. Crowther, *Biblical Servant Leadership*, Christian Faith Perspectives in
Leadership and Business, https://doi.org/10.1007/978-3-319-89569-7

Church, xvi, 2, 9, 15, 16, 18, 19, 23, 30, 34, 97–101, 106, 107, 111–114, 116–122, 124, 127, 148, 149, 154, 155, 158–165

Critique, 9, 34, 36, 39, 76, 93, 97, 131, 135, 140, 145, 163

Culture, xiv, 3, 8, 14, 16–18, 20–23, 28–30, 35, 76, 90, 92, 145, 149, 160

D

Destructive, 130

E

Effective, xiv, 2–4, 20, 21, 23, 28–29, 31, 35, 44, 49–51, 62, 63, 66, 69, 70, 104, 105, 109–112, 116, 118, 120, 123, 125, 127, 129, 130, 137, 139, 141, 145, 149, 162–165

Empowerment, 5, 26, 105, 147

Encounter, xvi, 44–51, 77, 110, 148, 156

Ethics, 4, 25, 28, 29, 35, 138, 147, 159

Example, xv, 18, 23, 34, 41–53, 57, 63, 75, 78, 84–87, 89–93, 97, 98, 100–104, 114–116, 118, 119, 125, 127, 137, 139, 142, 145, 150, 158, 159, 161, 163

Expansion, 23, 34, 42, 87, 97, 120, 131, 136, 140, 155

External, xv, 6, 30, 82, 91, 103, 108, 110, 119, 120, 130, 146, 156

F

Faith, 64, 88, 107, 108, 124, 142, 145, 156

Family, 30, 43, 75, 118, 121, 122, 156

Forgiveness, 43, 136, 146

Future, 15, 34, 42, 43, 48, 54, 76, 105, 109, 111, 123, 131, 138, 139, 144, 145, 148, 150, 155, 158, 159, 164, 165

G

Gentile, 51, 59, 78–81, 88, 98, 106

Gifts, 5, 16, 18, 50, 51, 82, 92, 105, 106, 109–114, 124, 140–143, 145, 147, 161

Global, 21–22

Great, 4, 6, 7, 15, 17, 21, 27, 33, 41, 42, 46, 61–64, 70, 72, 77–80, 85, 86, 88, 99, 100, 139, 150, 154, 158

Guidance, 9, 26, 138, 140, 147

Guiding, 87, 90

H

Heart, 2, 7, 23, 25, 50, 53, 58, 59, 62, 66, 70, 77, 102, 104, 136–139, 143, 144, 158

Hermeneutics, xvi, 39

Hope, 2, 26, 43, 54, 61, 104, 109, 112, 127, 136, 142, 144, 145

Humility, 5–8, 14, 26, 33, 44, 45, 47, 49–52, 60, 62–64, 71, 90–92, 98, 99, 101–103, 105, 110–116, 121–124, 126, 128, 136, 137, 140, 141, 145, 147–149, 154, 156

I

Inductive Bible study, 40, 78
Inner texture, 40, 44, 66, 68, 78, 82,
    84, 85, 87, 91, 101, 104,
    117–119, 142, 160
Integrity, xv, 7, 42, 43, 50, 119, 120,
    122, 123, 136, 140, 146
Internal, xv, 6, 7, 26, 28, 29, 31, 47,
    49, 65, 71, 80, 91, 93, 106,
    107, 110, 115, 116, 119, 120,
    123, 125, 130, 135, 136, 139,
    146–150, 156, 159, 164
Intertexture, 40, 86

J

Jesus, xiii–xv, 3, 8, 19, 21, 23, 27,
    29, 33, 41, 54, 72, 75–93, 97,
    100–102, 111, 112, 114–116,
    124–128, 135, 139–141, 143,
    145, 149, 150, 153–156, 159
Joy, 18, 43, 150

L

Leadership
    authentic, xiii, 3, 127, 128
    biblical, 39, 47, 50, 72, 88, 89,
        93, 128, 130, 131, 140–142,
        150, 153–165
    biblical servant, 20, 54, 72, 83,
        87, 93, 97, 128, 131,
        135–150, 154, 156, 164
    narcissistic, 128, 129, 149, 164
    servant, xiii–xv, 1–10, 13–23,
        25–36, 39–72, 75–93,
        97–131, 135–140, 145–149,
        154, 160, 161, 163, 164
    transformational, xiv, 6, 13, 14,
        19, 30, 31, 97, 127, 154, 155

Leadership development, xiv, xvi, 3,
    4, 14, 28, 30–32
Love, 5–7, 16, 17, 26, 29, 33, 41,
    84–87, 108–110, 112, 114,
    117, 123, 124, 128, 136, 137,
    141–148, 157
Luther, Martin, xiv, 15, 77, 108

M

Machiavelli, N., xv, 1, 129
Manipulation, 130
Maturity, 16, 17, 114, 116, 122,
    123, 140
Mission, 14, 18, 21, 26, 34, 46, 50,
    82, 83, 93, 104, 106, 128,
    138, 154, 156, 158
Moses, xiii, 44–51, 55, 59, 63, 70,
    72, 89, 137, 139, 147,
    156, 158
Motive, 7, 21, 25–27, 31, 85, 86,
    90, 102, 103, 107, 115, 125,
    126, 128, 130, 135, 136, 139,
    148, 157, 159

N

New Testament, xv, 9, 29, 41, 54,
    62, 64, 72, 75, 97–131, 135,
    140, 150, 154–156, 160, 164

O

Old Testament, xv, 9, 39–72, 81,
    86, 87, 101, 103, 125, 126,
    135, 138, 140, 153, 155,
    160, 164
Ontological, xv, 6, 27, 30, 80, 106,
    116, 117, 128, 136, 139, 146
Overseer, 90, 115, 117–119

**P**

Paul, xiv, 43, 89, 90, 93, 97–100,
    102–118, 137, 139–145,
    153–156, 158, 160–162
Peter, xiv, xv, 84–87, 89–90, 92, 97,
    100–104, 124–127, 137, 140,
    153, 155, 161
Plato, 1
Power, 1, 25, 26, 32, 35, 49, 51, 52,
    58, 60, 64, 65, 77, 88, 91, 92,
    102, 105, 115, 125–127, 129,
    130, 137, 140, 154
Prophet, 16, 54, 56–57, 61, 65–66,
    68, 69, 86, 112, 113, 141

**R**

Role model, 8, 28, 31–33, 75, 78,
    99, 102, 115, 124

**S**

Sacred texture, 40, 48, 49
Scripture(s), ix, xiii–xvi, 3, 6, 9, 10, 15,
    16, 34–36, 39, 40, 44, 48, 59,
    64, 71, 72, 79, 85, 88, 89, 91,
    93, 97, 111, 114, 115, 135–137,
    140–143, 145, 146, 150,
    153–155, 158, 160–162, 164
Self-exaltation, 61, 62, 64, 65, 69,
    72, 77, 137, 139
Self-focus, 21, 26, 43, 61–63, 65, 100,
    105, 125, 136–139, 149, 164
Service, 5, 8, 14, 16, 18, 25–27, 33,
    44, 51, 54–58, 71, 81, 83,
    109, 114, 136, 147, 156, 158
Shepherd, 53–54, 56, 57, 61, 62,
    66–69, 71, 72, 86, 87, 89, 90,
    93, 101–104, 124–126, 138,
    139, 141, 154, 155, 164

Social and cultural texture, 40, 92
Socio-rhetorical interpretation, 40,
    48, 78, 86, 92, 142
Spiritual, xiii, xiv, 3, 46, 84, 88, 98,
    103, 105, 107, 110, 112, 113,
    118, 140, 141, 143, 146,
    155, 164
Spirituality, xiii–xv, 3, 115, 141, 155,
    156, 159
Strategy, 7, 63, 122, 123, 128,
    140, 155
Success, 7, 28–30, 65, 70, 128–130,
    139, 147, 149, 150, 162–164
Successor, 70, 139, 147
Suffering, 42, 43, 54–55, 71, 89,
    90, 104, 105, 108, 109, 112,
    113, 124, 136, 144, 146, 148,
    149, 154

**T**

Toxic, 128, 149
Trust, 5, 7, 8, 14, 26, 33, 136, 144,
    147, 156

**V**

Virtues/virtuous, 1, 3–8, 10, 14, 16,
    26–29, 31–33, 35, 50, 52, 81,
    93, 104, 113, 119, 120, 123,
    129, 135, 136, 146, 147
Vision, 5–7, 14, 18, 26, 33–35,
    42, 46, 50, 67, 76, 90, 99,
    105, 127–129, 147, 150,
    154, 159

**W**

Wisdom, xv, 21, 30, 58, 70, 76,
    138, 147

CPSIA information can be obtained
at www.ICGtesting.com
Printed in the USA
LVOW13*1949210618
581517LV00011B/334/P